The Shape of Living

The Shape of Living

Spiritual Directions for Everyday Life

David F. Ford

CANTERBURY
PRESS
Norwich

© David F. Ford 2012

This edition published in 2012 by the Canterbury Press Norwich
Editorial office
3rd Floor, Invicta House,
108–114 Golden Lane,
London EC1Y 0TG

First published in Great Britain in 1997 by Fount Paperbacks.

Canterbury Press is an imprint of Hymns Ancient & Modern Ltd
(a registered charity)
www.canterburypress.co.uk

British Library Cataloguing in Publication data

A catalogue record for this book is available
from the British Library

978 1-84825-247-9
Kindle edition: 978 1-84825-289-6

Printed and bound by
CPI Group (UK) Ltd, Croydon, CR0 4YY

CONTENTS

For my wife Deborah, her mother and father Perrin and Dan, my mother Phyllis, and my friends Micheal and his wife Brid, dear companions in shaping life together; and in memory of Murray Cox.

PREFACE

It is good to see this new UK edition of *The Shape of Living*. In writing this book fifteen years ago, I attempted to sum up a whole approach to life, distilling years of experience, study, thought and conversation. A friend once said to me: 'You speak heart to heart in it, and fly free without having to worry about the academic footnotes and arguments.' That is not quite how it felt from the inside. The book was certainly written to a deadline – the result of having accepted the Archbishop of Canterbury's invitation to write it as his 'Lent book', but without really taking in how soon it had to be delivered. It was a difficult period in my life (I notice, on re-reading it, many signals of this) so the theme of being 'multiply overwhelmed' came naturally. The hours at the computer were snatched from days with many pressures, often early in the morning or late at night, and there were times of blockage and wrestling which felt the opposite of flying free. Yet it was liberating to be thinking as directly as possible about what matters most in life, and to reach out to a wide audience.

But the deeper secret of the book lay in the group (mentioned in the Introduction) who accompanied its writing, together with the wider circle of family, friends and colleagues who contributed at vital points. The group was mainly from the church where I was a member, together with some others from around Cambridge. Sharing the work in progress with them was an extraordinary experience. A majority of the group was in their sixties or older

(reflected now in the fact that, of those mentioned in the Acknow-
ledgements, five have died). Together they represented hundreds of
years of Christian living. Whenever I had a chapter ready they gathered and responded to it. I did my best to open up to their gentle but
firm and penetrating judgment, the weighing of my words against
their experience and wisdom. I remember two of the initial drafts
were rejected at once and had to be rewritten – not so much because
the group said so, as because, in the face of their questions and
reservations, it became clear to me that the drafts simply would
not do.

There was the wider set of conversations too, often intense. Of
those partners in the writing, several have also died. I choose just a
few for mention here, each of whom has had continuing influence
on more recent developments in the shape of my life and work.

Murray Cox, one of those to whom the book is dedicated, had
spent over twenty years working in Broadmoor (a high-security
psychiatric hospital) as a psychotherapist and psychiatrist, working
mostly with psychotic patients who had committed violent crimes.
We spent many hours in conversation, often together with my wife,
Deborah, and his collaborator and co-author, Alice Theilgaard. At
the time of Murray's death Alice, he and I were exploring together
writing a book on 'secrets', with particular reference to religion and
psychotherapy, and this was opening further dimensions of themes
in *The Shape of Living*. One of the most striking features of his
work was the use of drama, in particular Shakespeare (he and Alice
wrote *Shakespeare as Prompter: The Amending Imagination and
the Therapeutic Process*[1]), and I vividly remember sitting among
the patients of Broadmoor at the performance there of *Macbeth* by

---

[1] Murray Cox and Alice Theilgaard, *Shakespeare as Prompter: The Amending
Imagination and the Therapeutic Process* (Jessica Kingsley, London and Bristol, PA,
1994).

Mark Rylance and his company. Murray's passion for Shakespeare has for me since combined with other elements to make drama a leading theme for thinking and writing, to the extent that the sequel to *The Shape of Living*, which is at present being written, will be called *The Drama of Living*.

Donald (A.M.) Allchin, who has also died, was a priest, theologian, spiritual writer and, for me and many others, a wise mentor and encourager. He was an enthusiast for many things, two of which have been especially significant for me. One is the writing of Thomas Traherne (c.1637–1674) who is, I think, one of the greatest English Christian thinkers, and an exemplar of key topics and ideas in *The Shape of Living*. The other is the L'Arche communities for those with learning disabilities. Donald, Frances Young and the founder of L'Arche, Jean Vanier, joined in convening a group of theologians, including myself, at the mother community in Trosly-Breuil, France. For me this led into a long term, formative relationship with L'Arche. This appears briefly in *The Shape of Living* but has been more prominent in recent works, especially in *Christian Wisdom: Desiring God and Learning in Love*.[2] The engagement with L'Arche will be taken further in *The Drama of Living*.

Conversation with Daniel W. Hardy, father-in-law, colleague and co-writer, was of inestimable importance for *The Shape of Living*. But perhaps the deepest impression was made by the way he faced death during six months in 2007. The story is told in *Wording a Radiance: Parting Conversations on God and the Church*.[3] That

---

2 David F. Ford, *Christian Wisdom: Desiring God and Learning in Love* (Cambridge University Press, Cambridge, 2007), especially Chapter 10 'An interpersonal wisdom: L'Arche, learning disability and the Gospel of John'.

3 Daniel W. Hardy with Deborah Hardy Ford, Peter Ochs and David Ford, *Wording a Radiance: Parting Conversations on God and the Church*, (SCM, London, 2010).

has opened up further dimensions of several chapters in *The Shape of Living*, especially Chapter 6 on Evil, Suffering and Death, and these too will be explored in *The Drama of Living*.

Happily Micheal O'Siadhail is still alive and writing. One might say that *The Shape of Living* is immersed in both the Bible and his poetry. That interplay too has been a continuing feature of the intervening years, thanks to the remarkable collections of poems he has since published – *The Gossamer Wall, Love Life, Globe, and Tongues* .[4] Poetry, with its potential for combining head and heart, density of meaning with musicality, is for me the core form of human language. A moving aspect of responses to *The Shape of Living* over the years has been the number of readers who have been introduced to O'Siadhail's poetry and continue to read it.

Finally, it is especially good to have this edition because, whilst in the USA the book has always been available, and well served by Baker Books, here it has been out of print for many years. I am most grateful to Natalie Watson for being determined to publish it again in the UK and for overcoming several obstacles in order to do so. My great thanks also are due to Frances Clemson, who as my Research Associate has in this, as in so many other matters, offered both efficient assistance and wise judgment.

DAVID F. FORD
Cambridge, Summer 2012

---

4 These collections are all published by Bloodaxe Books, Tarsat: *The Gossamer Wall: Poems in Witness to the Holocaust* (2002); *Love Life* (2005); *Globe* (2007); and *Tongues* (2010).

COPING WITH BEING OVERWHELMED: HOW ARE OUR LIVES SHAPED?

While writing this book I asked a group of people what they found most overwhelming.

The first, a computer software designer, spoke of her new job and the sheer quantity of information, skills and recent developments she is expected to take in. She always feels inadequate, younger people seem to know far more than she does, and she is never able to catch up. A husband and wife talked about uncertainty in both their jobs. The wife has a contract with less than a year to run; the husband is already at the end of his, with nothing else in the pipeline. He feels overwhelmed by a pile of job applications. 'We want to get a cat, but we aren't sure we can afford it next year.' A doctor spoke about feeling overwhelmed by the pain, and sometimes despair, of his patients. An older woman said she is confused and feels quite unable to cope with the pace of change and all there is to keep up with. Others mentioned severe deafness, multiple responsibilities, financial insecurity, and a life-long, losing battle against overeating.

There were not only bad overwhelmings. Someone had been to the Canadian Rockies and described the impact of the beauty and the vastness. An Indian spoke passionately about the good and the bad together. She said that in India in recent years millions more have sunk below the poverty line, and she was angry about the things that contributed to this. But it was more complicated than that. She also talked about the extraordinary generosity she has experienced in the midst of poverty, and the overwhelming gratitude expressed for small things. Later in the conversation she described in poetic detail a recent encounter with an adder – the sheer beauty of the snake.

So it went on. There were fourteen people, and these were only the things they would share in a group that size – we all knew that there was much more that could have come out. But it was still quite a list: information and knowledge overload, financial and job insecurity, responsibilities, overeating, pain, despair, beauty, confusion, inadequacy, poverty, generosity and gratitude. Most were only mentioning one overwhelming – but life is not that simple.

This book is about coping with multiple overwhelmings, both good and bad. I see this as the most important thing in our lives. The basic question is: how, in the midst of all our overwhelmings, are our lives shaped?

In this introduction I will suggest three imperatives for us as we try to respond to being overwhelmed, and will offer two images of it: the computer and the flood. Then I will raise the crucial questions that the following seven chapters will be exploring. Finally, I will look at the religions as resources for coping with being overwhelmed.

RESPONDING TO BEING OVERWHELMED:
THREE IMPERATIVES

The group discussion reported above underlines the huge variety of experiences that might come under the heading of being overwhelmed. The combinations are endless, and there are no simple recipes for coping. But I hope this book might help readers in responding, and I begin with three guidelines which underlie my own approach.

Name it!

The first essential is to name it. 'I am overwhelmed!' It is amazing how liberating it can be, even when all our overwhelmings seem to be bad ones, simply to acknowledge the fact. Naming is a powerful act. It can be even more transformative when we name something that is as hard to define as multiple overwhelming. By definition we cannot get outside our overwhelmings to inspect them, assess them and work out a cool response. To name the situation brings it into language. Language is shared, and to find just the right word links our experience to others. The gift of a name lets us find a perspective in which we can start 'coming to terms' with our situation by talking about it – to ourselves in our own thoughts, and to others.

Describe it!

The next step is to try to describe it. As soon as we begin this we glimpse how common our situation is. Being overwhelmed in several ways can be the most isolating of experiences. We struggle against drowning in the bad overwhelmings, and often feel guiltily responsible for not being on top of our situation. Describing it, like naming it, links us to other people. We realize how many people this category fits. Indeed, we see that it is actually very human and quite normal to be complexly over-whelmed. Describing it frees us from the wrong sort of guilt and from paralysing isolation. It also helps in countering the response of despair. A common reaction when we can see no way out is to feel that it is all too much, and to be tempted to give up. Describing it as a 'normal' problem does not solve it, but it does create a solidarity in which the isolation of our despair is challenged.

But how to describe something so complex, multifaceted and intense? I will draw on many sources and disciplines, ranging through history and around the world, to try to do justice to our multiple overwhelmings. But there are two sources that will be drawn on continually, interwoven as the ground bass of the book. One is the Bible, and I have found it yielding all sorts of fresh insights in response to the question: what does the Bible say about being multiply overwhelmed? The other is the poetry of Micheal O'Siadhail, whose powerful and accessible poems distil an immense amount of wisdom on the themes of this book. I find the current expanding popularity of poetry very important: the more overwhelming life becomes, the more we need the creativity of the best minds and imaginations. Poetry at its best has wrestled with the great overwhelmings, and out of that engagement has shaped a language through which we too can respond.

Good description also guards against inadequate responses. One of the commonest temptations is the simple solution. Sometimes this tackles head-on one form of overwhelming while ignoring the others – as if it is a wise solution to cope with money problems at the expense of family life or justice. Perceptive description reveals how a life is like an ecology. The various forms of overwhelming are all parts of a whole. To deal with one part separately without taking account of the rest throws all the dynamics out of balance. So the next guideline follows.

Attend to the Shape of Living!

The issue at stake is the whole shape of living. To attend to that when we are being overwhelmed is no easy matter. But it is hard to imagine any adequate way of coping that does not try to answer the big questions about life, death, purpose, good and evil. So the basic conviction of this book is that we need to attend to the shape of living. We do not need to drown in what overwhelms us. Nor is the solution to fiddle with some of the details, important though they are. While doing justice to both the overwhelmings and the details, the main task is to stretch our minds, hearts and imaginations in trying to find and invent shapes of living. It is a task as old as the flood and as modern as the computer.

COPING WITH THE COMPUTER

Faced with a new software package for word processing how do we cope?

Even to have got as far as settling on one package among the dozens on offer is an achievement. If we are in a business or institution we are often relieved to follow its lead and buy the one they use. But, having got it and loaded it on to the computer, there is the process of immersion, which can easily feel like drowning. Usually there is a Tutor, introducing the program in 'easy' lessons, and a Manual (mine is 816 pages) in which anything can be looked up (if we know the right terms). The wise learner takes a few days to get acquainted with the basics and then tries to build on them. But who has a few days to spare? Other things press, and even if we do take those precious days it is not always easy to decide what the basics are for us. A good program can carry out a vast variety of operations, but most of them might be useless for the sort of work we want to do. It is common to feel overwhelmed by the complexities, by the bewildering possibilities, and by the frustrations of failing time and again to get the results we want.

The other side of this overwhelming experience is the knowledge that there is no such thing as an insignificant detail in the program. Every touch on the keyboard matters, every dot and space. Leaving things undone can be as disastrous as doing the wrong thing. We press the wrong key and lose a day's work, with the added guilty awareness that we should have guarded in advance against losing it. Often our fingers have learnt their own habits from other software or keyboards, so we have to unlearn and learn at the same time.

So there we are, inundated by possibilities and yet having to strike the next key. Somehow, through much trial and error, we usually work out how to make 'good enough' use of the program. We expand our repertoire of commands, learn how to avoid serious mistakes, and start producing texts (after getting the printer to work). We build up experience and get into habits so that we make the program our own. We use it for our purposes and it shapes our work practices and options.

What has happened? We have been overwhelmed. We have paid attention to detail. And somehow a small part of our living has been shaped as we have tried to cope with both the overwhelming and the details.

THE FLOOD AND OTHER INUNDATIONS

The classic Jewish and Christian story about this (with many parallels in other ancient Near Eastern religions) is of Noah's ark and the flood. It has a primordial power to speak to generation after generation, and it continues to inspire new variations and interpretations.

When faced with inundation Noah builds an ark. It requires great attention to detail ('the length of the ark three hundred cubits, its breadth fifty cubits, and its height thirty cubits...' – Genesis 6:15), and it is shaped into a boat that saves some humans and other creatures from drowning.

The story opens with a world inundated by wickedness. The subsiding of the flood is followed by God's embracing blessing and unconditional covenant, with the overarching beauty of the rainbow as its sign. The multiple overwhelmings of evil, catastrophe, blessing and beauty give room and reason for the building of the ark. There have been many ark-builders down the centuries: those who have faced bad overwhelmings, and who have nevertheless helped to form lives and communities that are even more radically shaped by the good overwhelmings.

The ending of the story of Noah is, however, a reminder of the apparently endless capacity of life to produce further forms of overwhelming: 'Noah was the first tiller of the soil. He planted a vineyard; and he drank of the wine, and became drunk, and lay uncovered in his tent ...' (Genesis 9:20–21). Drunkenness is still high among the world's ways of being habitually overwhelmed. There are frequent new addictions. A survey of users of the worldwide web in New York discovered that it was rapidly becoming a form of addiction: 17 per cent of those surveyed were on-line for purposes other than their work for over 40 hours a week.

So, in between the flood and the computer, human history is shaped by many overwhelmings. There are some continuous strands – sex, money, power, violence, knowledge, pleasure, responsibility. There are the huge events – a war, a massacre, a stock market collapse, an AIDS epidemic, the birth of a new nation, public events which affect millions and change the course of groups and nations. Or there are more personal events – falling in love; the birth of a child; divorce; serious illness; finding or losing a job; bereavement.

We tell the stories of our lives around such events. We try to deal with them at the same time as coping with all the other overwhelming phenomena. We often fail to cope, at least by the standards of success set up by us or by our families or by others. The failure itself becomes a complex event in our lives. We may end up in psychiatric care, or take to drink or drugs or overeating (the main forms of 'substance overwhelming' in our culture). The forms of escapism in response to bad types of overwhelming are endlessly varied. Some do it in a more 'internal' way, such as living a fantasy life, or becoming depressed. Others externalize it in hectic activities, anger, aggression, and many ways of 'taking it out on other people'. All these responses in turn generate more events.

So the consequences of multiple overwhelming create more intensive overwhelming. One mother who cannot cope has consequences for husband, children and others. Families, groups and whole nations can be drawn into spirals of responses, which spread and complexify. The personal and the political interact, so do the local and the global, the economic and the cultural. It is like a vast, multi-levelled ecology in which everything is somehow related to everything else. An event in one niche sends ripples through all the others. In the public sphere the speed of reporting an event intensifies the ripples and can make them into waves. Soon one local event has become a crisis.

Crisis is the term for an event which is judged (but who makes the judgement?) to be of overwhelming importance. The urgency of a crisis takes over the present moment and demands attention and action. In a world of multiple overwhelming and rapid communication by media which thrive on reporting (and creating) 'events', public life is bound to appear like continual crisis management. Life in workplaces, in organizations of all sorts, and even in families, can easily feel like that too. Each sphere of life is bombarded by information, 'issues to be taken seriously', and demands for higher performance and more accountability. Or else we are not subject to those demands and feel useless, marginalized, ignored or bored.

In all of this the shaping or distorting of our lives goes on. We tend to feel that our own modern period is special – surely we are subject to unprecedented overwhelmings? That may be true, but it gives all the more importance to the need to draw on the pre-modern wisdom in this area. I suspect that most periods have, from the inside, felt multiply overwhelming. They have certainly had to cope with sex, money, power, death and so on, as well as cataclysmic events. One of the good things about our 'late-modern' or 'post-modern' situation is that many of us have rejected modernity's superiority complex, which has often disdained the pre-modern in the name of progress. Now we are free in a new way to recognize what is of value in pre-modernity, modernity and post-modernity. So we can range from the flood to the computer in our search for life-shaping wisdom.

THE SHAPE OF THIS BOOK

Our lives may be formed more radically through the questions that grip us than through particular answers – and any worthwhile answer will raise new questions. Each chapter of this book is conceived as a response to life-shaping questions. Even if a reader finds that some of the suggested answers do not strike a chord, I hope the questions will be valuable and fascinating enough to encourage further searching and meditation.

Chapter 1, 'Faces and Voices – Shaping a Heart', asks about the most important people in our lives. The main form of over-whelming is by people. Who are the faces and voices that concern us daily? Who are the people from the past and present who are always in our hearts, even when we are not thinking of them? Before whom do we live? Who is welcomed and who is shut out? Whom do we try to please? Whom do we fear? How is the heart of our identity shaped by these people?

Chapter 2, 'Vocations and Compulsions – Life-Shaping Desires', is about the longings, callings, passions, obsessions and long-term orientations that are the leading themes in our lives. What are our deepest desires? What promises and commitments shape the drama of our lives? What is our vocation? How might we discover it?

Chapter 3, 'Power, Virtue and Wisdom – The Shaping of Character', asks about the secret of real goodness. Why do we feel a shock of surprise and delight at it? Can we take Jesus's call to perfection seriously? Where do we find the power to have the great virtues such as love, faith, hope, courage, patience and gentleness? Where do we find the wisdom needed to lead respon-sible yet joyful lives? How might this wisdom be learnt?

Chapter 4, 'Secrets and Disciplines – Soul-Shaping', explores the formation of our most intimate selves. Why is secrecy a crucial part of coping with being overwhelmed in intimacy with other people and with God? What are the disciplines of intimacy? How do we cope with so much of ourselves being hidden even from ourselves? What are the 'practices of excess' that can help cope with overwhelming mystery? What about the secrets and disciplines of communities as well as individuals? And how do we face the mystery of death?

Chapter 5, 'Leisure and Work – Shaping Time and Energy', looks at the rhythm of our days, weeks and years. What is the wisdom of the sabbath? How do we work in an economy overwhelmed by global competition, flooded with knowledge and information, and obsessive about money as the 'bottom line' for everything? How is God involved in the dynamic network of exchanges of money, goods, services, energy, knowledge and information? What about the work of creating and sustaining organizations and institutions? How might we manage our time better?

Chapter 6, 'Knocked Out of Shape – Evil, Suffering and Death', is about the worst overwhelmings. How can we be held in our suffering? What can we learn from those who have suffered intensely and come through? What about compassion? And healing? Can faith in God face the terrible interrogation of evil, suffering and death? Is it conceivable that death itself could be overwhelmed?

Chapter 7, 'Kaleidoscope – Resurrection, Joy and Feasting', is about the best overwhelmings. Joy which seems too good to be true is seen as an even greater scandal than evil, suffering or death. The chapter asks first about the resurrection and its invitation to trust a God of joy. Then it explores the experience of feasting and hospitality, not only with actual food and drink but also with the mind and the imagination. How can we feast on beauty and truth? Then finally there is the hospitality of God, which is developed through the ancient image of the dance, brought up to date through O'Siadhail's poetry of dance, and culminating in a 'vertigo of gladness'.

RESOURCES FOR COPING: THE RELIGIONS

Where might we find resources to answer such questions? Clearly there is a need to look in a wide variety of places, and that is what we will be doing. But the religions, both historically or as realities in the world today, are undoubtedly the primary place of both the overwhelming and the shaping of lives. I see them as 'homes' and 'schools' in which lives are formed. They are homes and schools for communities, peoples and even civilizations, but also for many individuals who stand out against the pressures of groups, or who try to cope in relative isolation.

Most major religious communities have deep roots in pre-modern periods. They also have cumulative traditions that have come through many centuries and have survived successive crises and catastrophes. They have spanned languages, cultures, economic systems and civilizations. In all these interactions they have both undergone and enabled life-shaping transformations. This process is now being intensified globally.

Probably about four billion people around the world today are directly involved in a major religion. Many others are influenced by one or more religious traditions. The most obvious way our world is being affected at present is through a large number of bloody conflicts with religious dimensions. But that is just the tip of the iceberg. One reason for those conflicts is that religions (like families, the greatest single arena of conflict) go so deep – to the very heart of people's identity. No area of life is outside their concern. They offer immense resources for life-shaping, but for that very reason they have terrible destructive power – 'the corruption of the best is the worst'.

But there is a problem with taking religion as something useful for resourcing our lives. That way of seeing it at our service contradicts what is characteristic of most religions: they are about us being at the service of God or some reality other than ourselves. The inside experience of faith, for example, is often of being overwhelmed by the reality of God. This can take many forms: intellectual amazement at a God 'than which none greater can be conceived'; imaginative and emotional response to abundant glory, goodness or love; practical dedication to a whole way of life with others. In most faiths, worship is the activity which shows this clearly and repeatedly. Worship is a habit which copes with being overwhelmed by God.

Worship and similar activities – any involvement which calls for all we have and are – is therefore a constant theme of this book. That is where we look for some of the deepest wisdom about coping with being multiply overwhelmed. The conclusion will be that the wisest way to cope is not to try to avoid being overwhelmed, and certainly not to expect to be in control of everything; rather it is to live amidst the overwhelmings in a way that lets one of them be the overwhelming that shapes the others. That is the 'home' or 'school' in which the practicalities of coping can be learnt.

WHICH RELIGION?

But which religion? As the religions have interacted more, especially in the twentieth century, they have become one of the most challenging forms of multiple overwhelming. The heart of the problem is that each religion is a radical, life-embracing involvement. As a whole way of life it is incompatible with other religions or quasi-religions.

This is only partly a matter of beliefs and truth claims. These do pose huge issues which are probably irreconcilable. Yet it is possible to find in most religions those who do not see their own beliefs necessarily ruling out the possibility of salvation (or whatever their tradition's equivalent for 'salvation' might be) for those of other faith traditions and none. More radically, the acuteness of the problem is due to its being a question of what I have been calling the shape of living. Someone involved in a lifetime of faithful Muslim practice cannot also be committed to a lifetime of faithful Jewish practice. The same is even more obviously true for whole worshipping communities. Of course a Muslim may be deeply influenced by Jews and Judaism, and in deep relationships of understanding and friendship to the point of being 'bilingual' in both traditions. But it is very hard to imagine anyone genuinely carrying out the core practices and holding the core beliefs of both faiths simultaneously without falling into contradictions, falling out with one or both communities, or in effect founding a new hybrid religious community.

Even religions or quasi-religions with apparently looser identities, such as some 'mix and match' forms of New Age religion, meet the same problem. However many truth questions are left to one side, and however tolerantly open the boundaries are, in fact these lifestyles generate certain shapes of living which are incompatible with others.

It is probable that in practice the religion of many in our society could be described as a form of polytheism: there are many shifting objects of esteem and desire, many beliefs, many 'gods' demanding 'worship' in explicit or implicit forms, and time and energy are divided among these 'cults'. People in this position sometimes feel at an advantage over those committed to more single-minded faiths, seeing themselves as more open, flexible and pragmatic. That is debatable; but what is clear is that they do not avoid having a particular shape of living. Even a claim to impartiality, neutrality or flexibility in the face of religious options is itself a definite and controversial option.

How is the situation of many religions and quasi-religions best handled? The great questions about life-shaping truth, beauty and practice do not allow for neutral treatments. Everybody stands somewhere! Nobody has a God's-eye overview, and our own position needs to be open to question and discussion. The best engagements are between those who can say where they are coming from and then patiently try to communicate and discuss matters of importance. This by no means rules out deep differences – in fact it guarantees them. But, as chapter 1 will suggest, how our 'community of the heart' is hospitable towards those who differ most from us is the best test of its quality.

In this book I will try to explain where I come from, and discuss the big questions raised in this introduction. I will not, however, be concerned with comparing religions. I am privileged to work in a university faculty where Jews, Christians, Muslims, Buddhists, Hindus, and others with no specific allegiance learn and teach theology and religious studies together. That setting constantly stretches everyone's hospitality, wisdom and generosity. It also makes it clear that to try to do justice to even two of those faiths in comparison and contrast with one another would need a book far longer than this, and preferably in the form of a dialogue. So I do not attempt that here.

Instead, I try to speak out of one faith and let readers make comparisons. But the one at the heart of my faith is hospitable to all people. In a world increasingly aware of diversity and pluralism I imagine Jesus Christ saying: 'I am the difference.' And in the midst of all the other overwhelmings of this world, I hope that readers will accompany me through these chapters, which culminate at the end of the book in a vision of God that reaches back to the prophet Ezekiel:

> Then the Spirit lifted me up, and as the glory of the Lord arose from its place, I heard behind me the sound of a great earthquake; it was the sound of the wings of the living creatures as they touched one another, and the sound of the wheels beside them, that sounded like a great earthquake. The Spirit lifted me up and took me away, and I went in bitterness in the heat of my spirit, the hand of the Lord being strong upon me; and I came to the exiles at Tel-abib, who dwelt by the river Chebar. And I sat there overwhelmed among them seven days. (Ezekiel 3:12–15)

Being overwhelmed by God is the situation in which I have been gripped by the life-shaping questions in this book.

ONE

FACES AND VOICES – SHAPING A HEART

People are all around us, but they are also inside us. Each of us has a 'community of the heart' made up of those people who are most important for us. Of all the sources of overwhelming, people are the most significant. Our most powerful feelings relate to them, feelings such as love, anger, jealousy, hatred, rivalry, gratitude, hero worship, status seeking, and the urge to dominate. A big part of our inner life is taken up with people, and they loom large in our memories, fantasies and hopes. So the shape of our living is largely created by our relationships with people.

COMMUNITY OF THE HEART

'Heart' is a way of talking about that dimension of our self where memory, feeling, imagination and thinking come together. The heart is like a home for all the concerns of our lives, where our identity is sorted out year after year. Above all it is inhabited by images of other people and of ourselves in relation to them. Our hearts are filled with the faces and voices of those before whom we live. These are the members of our 'community of the heart'.

Some of them are so much part of our identity that they are woven into the texture of our feeling and thinking. Their voices in

1

us may not be distinguishable from what we habitually say to ourselves.

Others continually confront us. The thought of them may cause fear, resentment or shame. They may represent a joy, a bereavement, a call to higher things, a challenge, or the 'voice of conscience'.

Most of us can, for example, look back on our lives and think of people decisive in encouraging us. Micheal O'Siadhail writes of a teacher in 'Foster-Figure':

> Even now there is some enigma
> in that glance. Though long grown
> beyond a first self-surrender
> or cooler reappraisals, I prize
> his affirmation, always revere him.

Years later this teacher has become part of him, and the encouraging glance and words go on providing energy and inspiration:

> I probe the essence of this energy;
> no blandishments or blind approval,
> his unblinking trust enticed me,
> fingered some awareness of worth;
> in his praise all is possible.

> Though at first a copy-cat tremor,
> after many storms I'll still
> strum the chord of his assurance,
> that music I'll make my own,
> an old resonance I'll summon up.[1]

The other side of that is the discouragement, the people who undermine us. O'Siadhail finds that too, in the same school after staff changes:

> New brooms with fresh sweeps.
> How easily we become how we're seen;
> Failure throws an oblong shadow,
> I cover hurts with jaunty humour,
>
> pretend not to care, affect disdain,
> harden the core to day-by-day
> humiliations – tiny erosions of respect –
> learn the slow rustings of shame.
>
> And laugh a bitter laugh!…
>
> How many faces must a wound wear?[2]

THE HEART – HABITABLE AND HOSPITABLE

That is how hearts are shaped – by the music of voices we make our own and by wounds with many faces. To ask 'Who am I?' leads straight to the other people who are part of me. Is there any layer of self where there are no others? We find ourselves partly by remembering those who are the most deeply woven into us and by continuing to relate to them. An experienced psychotherapist told me that a great deal of his work is to do with the quality of the 'community' that clients carry around inside them.

So it helps to think of ourselves as a sort of community. Each of us has a different set of people who inhabit our heart. To think of the heart as a home is not necessarily a cosy picture: there are peaceful, loving homes, but there are also many with divorce, violence and other miseries. There are limits to the picture – clearly we have to think of ourselves as individuals too, and that will be a concern of chapter 4 on the secrets and disciplines of soul-shaping. But the bias of our culture tends to play down the ways in which we are communities in ourselves. It is easy to ignore the fact that the very language we use in order to think about ourselves and to describe ourselves is learnt from others, and that at every crucial point we are shaped in relationships.

How do we discover the shape of our hearts? There are two basic ways. First, we can find out who are the leading members of our inner community. It begins as an exercise in naming the 'most significant others'. These are the people who indwell us, who are at the core of our 'home life' as a self. We always live in their presence, whether they are physically there or not. Whether our heart is habitable or not depends in large measure on our relationship with these people.

Second, we can look at the boundaries of our life. Besides the most significant others, all sorts of people figure in our heart's domestic drama. Often we have no choice about them – a new boss, colleague or neighbour, and the people we come up against as we move through many situations. But, even in those relationships which are simply given by the situations we find ourselves in, we are rarely passive. Our heart forms its habits of welcoming and rejecting. There are very different ways of being part of one heart's community. Its boundaries are not fixed and they can be more open or more closed. This is what I call the hospitality of the heart. How welcoming are we to different types of people? How willing are we to be given hospitality by others – or even to ask for it?

So two essential dynamics that shape our heart are its home life of deepest relationships, and its patterns of hospitality. They can be seen as two forms of overwhelming.

OVERWHELMED AT THE CORE

In one life it is rare that the really significant others number more than a handful. To name them is to name our most personal form of being overwhelmed. They are inside us as well as outside us. They may be on the other side of the world or they may be dead, but they are constantly before us and within us. They are so deep in us that we can never come to terms with them in any final way – we can never get them 'into perspective'.

Are there people without this experience? Some people seem to have nothing but bland, fairly neutral relationships. Or their feelings seem to be distributed in more or less equal portions among a large number of people. Or their passions do not seem to have to do with people at all. But it still seems true that most people are not like that. There is even some sense that being fully human involves the capacity to be overwhelmed in particular relationships. Otherwise we suspect some dimension is missing, or that it has been displaced or diverted into something else.

The key people come into our lives in many ways. The most common is by being family. The crucial relationships in a life, for better and for worse, are most likely to be with parents, grand-parents, brothers, sisters, husband, wife, children. Then there are those family-like relationships of partners, friends, enemies, and the members of any long-term group. And there can be endless surprises. Many of us know what it is like to be gripped by someone through a biography, a television programme, or a comparatively brief encounter, and sometimes these have profound, heart-shaping effects.

How do we cope with the overwhelming people at the core of our being? Much of the rest of this book is an attempt to answer that. The preparation for considering how to cope is to name our own key faces and voices and begin to discern how they shape our heart. What are our most vivid memories? What have been our crises and passions? Who figures most prominently in the drama of our inner life?

OVERWHELMED FROM ALL DIRECTIONS

How does our heart offer and receive hospitality? People converge on us in so many ways, in all areas of our life as well as through all the media. There is not even any need for them to be 'real'. One of the distinctive features of our culture is the large number of fictional people we interact with daily.

The characters in a long-running 'soap' about ordinary Londoners or Australians may become more significant than many members of our own family. The huge audiences for films and videos, and the millions of readers of novels, are 'being entertained' – the language of hospitality is appropriate. They are being drawn into a fictional world, and in turn are welcoming fictional people and plots into their lives. This is something of immense importance. Taking part in this fiction-saturated culture, we discover who we are and we test out our identities. We enter into the fictional worlds of novels, plays, films and all sorts of other stories. But the lines between fiction and reality are not at all clear, and our hopes, fears, dreams, and conceptions of reality may be more profoundly affected by fiction than by 'true stories' (if those are what historians and journalists tell).

Switching between fiction and real life is a sophisticated ability which children begin to learn young. As I write, across the passage my seven-year-old daughter, Rachel, is in her room by herself with her dolls. They each have names and roles, and she has a range of individual voices for the drama that is going on. My eleven-year-old daughter, Rebecca, is currently writing a story about a gang of children. Some of the characters were invented by her grandmother years ago, as bedtime stories in which my daughter also always figured; I later took over and introduced some more characters; and now she has them all on computer and is adding current friends and locations. These 'Paddy stories' have been going on for years, and interweave her life with fictional people and plots. Who can tell how fact and fiction relate in them? But that is not the most interesting question. More important are the quality of the stories, the shaping of imagination and the insight into people and herself.

Rebecca does not, of course, confuse the Alice in the stories with the Alice who comes to stay. The fact that she is trying to write about Alice acting 'in character' in a fictional adventure probably even helps to understand Alice in real life. There are obviously many times when it is important to separate fact from fiction. The critical matter is that Alice can actually be affected by what Rebecca believes to be true.

But the further we move from home the less easy it is to preserve the distinction between fact and fiction. We are inundated with 'real people' from around the world through the media. How are we to 'entertain' both Hollywood stars and the refugees of Rwanda? How do we work out our boundaries? To whom do we offer the hospitality of our heart? Sometimes it feels as if we have been invaded. But in so far as we do have a choice, who deserves our attention? Our money? Our vote? Our campaigning? Our prayer?

Every group and organization we are connected with adds faces and voices to the traffic in our hearts, and often invites us into responsibilities too. On our judgements and decisions hangs much of the shaping of our lives. But the quality of our decisions will substantially depend on the faces and voices before whom we live in our core community. And often the formative influences on that community in our heart have been overwhelming events.

HEART-OVERWHELMING EVENTS

Overwhelming relationships at the core, and hospitality across boundaries where huge numbers of real and imagined people press for admission: if those are the two most powerful dynamics of the heart then it is not surprising that our lives are most creatively or shatteringly transformed when they come together in one event. 'Falling in love' is a classic form of this, when a new person crosses the threshold of our life and overwhelms our core. Micheal O'Siadhail describes this in 'Out of the Blue':

Nothing can explain this adventure – let's say a quirk
of fortune steered us together – we made our covenants,
began this odyssey of ours, by hunch and guesswork,
a blind date where foolish love consented in advance.
No my beloved, neither knew what lay behind the frontiers.
You told me once you hesitated: A needle can waver,
then fix on its pole; I am still after many years
baffled that the needle's gift dipped in my favour.

Should I dare to be so lucky? Is it a dream?
Suddenly in the commonplace that first amazement seizes
me all over again – a freak twist to the theme,
subtle jazz of the new familiar, trip of surprises.
Gratuitous, beyond our fathom, both binding and freeing,
this love re-invades us, shifts the boundaries of our being.'

That is an event of mutual overwhelming. It distils some of the key marks of heart-transforming relationships: novelty, risk, trust, mystery, amazement, and coming to a joint understanding and commitment – 'we made our covenants'. The last two lines sum up the overwhelming by something 'beyond our fathom', and the reshaping of hearts as love 'shifts the boundaries of our being'.

When this happens it is never just one person who enters our heart: the other brings their whole community too. The sharing of our core communities with each other is one of the most important elements in a close relationship. It also raises classic problems about how the two core communities relate to each other – all those jokes about in-laws! The boundaries of our being continue to shift as each of us introduces new faces and voices, and the scope for border disputes is endless. The energy and will to cope with them are focused by that covenant of trust, and the gratitude and hope at its heart.

In our deepest mutual relationships we depend above all on those few people who, having said 'yes' to being overwhelmed by us, then allow that to go on shaping and reshaping their hearts year after year as 'love re-invades'.

THE INTRUSION OF THE FACELESS

But such mutuality is not all. We constantly meet with faces and voices which appeal to us to help, to have compassion, or to take some practical responsibility that goes beyond what our commitments or inclinations oblige us to do. These appeals cut across our friendships, marriages and in-groups. They pose one of the biggest questions to us and to our groups: how do we cope with the suffering of the poor, the hungry, the impaired, the marginalized, the victim? These may be the test of the right shaping of our hearts even more than friends, spouses or fellow group members. O'Siadhail's poem 'Intrusion' graphically describes how the relationship of mutual love can be broken open by 'the stricken'.

The glaze of loved and lover,
our amorous self-containment,
concentric and utterly present
to the other. Sweetest hour.

But what if between our gazes
shadows of the stricken fall,
the stares we seem to veil
keep on commanding us?

Our two-ness is never alone.
Whose is that intrusive face
that looms unseen between us
condemning all we haven't done?

The eclipsed. The destitute.
O sly worm of dominance

coiling its own discountenance,
our masks and blottings out.

Is love a threadbare blindfold?
'Yes,' say our shadows, 'unless
you turn to face the faceless.'
Who'll re-envisage the world?[4]

O'Siadhail is describing something fundamental to human life. It is easy to think that these intrusive faces are accidents, unfortunate people who disrupt 'normal' life. But in fact they go to the heart of who we are. This is because each person and each group has boundaries, and one of the easiest ways of making boundaries is by exclusion. We usually define ourselves over against other people and groups.

Children offer vivid examples of this: the recurring rivalries, peer group pressures, fears of rejection, worries about 'Who is my friend?' or 'Will I look a fool?' Adults are not too different. Groups naturally produce outsiders. This need not be a bad thing, as often outsiders have their own groups or may not want to belong to ours anyway. But many boundaries are only maintained by privilege, power or violence. And many people do not have habitable groups in which they can flourish. The most obvious are the destitute, refugees, displaced or persecuted. They act as test cases for our hospitality.

There are other dimensions to this. The stricken may not be so easily identifiable. There are so many other forms of exclusion which leave deep hurts. Our habits of exclusion may be learnt almost unconsciously from our family, race, class or religion. Or our hearts may be shaped by having been marginalized or victimized ourselves – that can make us sympathetic to others, but it can also make us more protective of our own boundaries, more threatened by outsiders.

The point is not that boundaries are wrong. Nor can we be expected to respond to every appeal, or to take every 'victim' at face value. It is rather about the shaping of our heart's habits. How can we not treat others as faceless? How do we avoid what O'Siadhail calls 'blottings out' of the needy? Can we live in the presence of the 'eclipsed' and genuinely face them? Can we really listen to voices of misery or agony?

Simone Weil thought that it is almost impossible to be in the presence of someone in deep affliction and pay them full, compassionate attention. We find ourselves wanting to escape. We blame the victim. We disown responsibility. We take some token action. We explain the affliction so as to put the responsibility elsewhere. We get on with urgent business. We allow ourselves to be distracted. And so on.

There are many ways of looking at life which see it as perfectly natural and right to harden our heart in such circumstances, unless we have some clear personal responsibility in the situation. Yet there are also persistent and powerful traditions of radical compassion, and these are clearest in the great religious traditions.

In the Jewish case, the formative events of their tradition built love for the outsider into the heart of their identity. The Israelites were foreigners and slaves in Egypt, and they were never to forget that. In the Bible, Deuteronomy binds together as closely as possible love for God and love for the one who does not belong to Israel:

And now, Israel, what does the Lord your God require of you, but to fear the Lord your God, to walk in all his ways, to love him, to serve the Lord your God with all your heart and with all your soul, and to keep the commandments and statutes of the Lord, which I command you this day for your good? ... He executes justice for the fatherless and the widow, and loves the sojourner, giving him food and clothing. Love the sojourner therefore; for you were sojourners in the land of Egypt. (Deuteronomy 10:12–19)

That gives the crucial guideline for how we exercise the hospitality of our heart. We are to follow 'the criterion of the vulnerable'. This does not mean that the faces of our family, friends, and others in our core community are excluded. But it does ask what other faces are there too. Who are the others in our inner drama? To whom else are we responsible? Can we risk the boundaries of our heart being overwhelmed by the needy once we pay them compassionate attention? Do we glimpse the astonishing truth that, before this God, the way we treat outsiders may be the single most important factor in the quality of our core community of insiders? The final question of 'Intrusion' hints at how high the stakes are here:

Who'll re-envisage the world?

It is the difference between a faceless world and one with a new 'visage' of hospitality and compassion, formed by responding to the appeal in the faces of the suffering. Such behaviour re-envisages the world.

THE WOUNDED HEART

But what if we are the vulnerable ones and are actually hurt? When someone deeply hurts us it is one of the worst forms of overwhelming. It can dominate a whole life, as often happens between parents and children. The one who has wounded us keeps coming into our thoughts, feelings and imaginings.

The extent of the misery is a measure of how vital other people are to us. Because others are so deeply part of us, when core relationships go wrong our whole being is threatened. We feel that the weave of our self with others is unravelling or being torn, patterns that have taken years to weave between us are destroyed, habits of trusting communication are betrayed. Similar traumas happen when we are hurt or rejected by a group or organization.

'How many faces must a wound wear?' In O'Siadhail's case when he was humiliated at school, those 'faces' included jaunty humour, bitter laughter, pretending not to care, hardening his core against 'tiny erosions of respect', and shame. It is no accident that shame is often seen in terms of the face. We 'daren't show our face', we lower our eyes, blush, feel looked down on. Shame has a way of polluting our heart. It feels like an ecological catastrophe of the self. Our whole personal environment is affected – how we are in our own eyes and in the eyes of others. It seems as if nothing will ever flourish again for us.

Then there is the other side of being hurt which is often insepar-able from it: hurting others. The wisdom of the religions is clear: by hurting others we wound our own heart more terribly than by anything others can inflict on us. This is almost unimaginable, to think that being nasty to someone is worse for us than suffering them being nasty to us. It is not true that the worst thing that can happen to us is being wronged, wounded or even killed: the worst thing is to do wrong. The double tragedy is that our wounds, which can be so terrible, are often an almost irresistible tempta-tion to inflict wounds on others. How had O'Siadhail's teachers been hurt?

These themes will be treated further in later chapters, especially those on power, virtue and wisdom and on evil, suffering and death. For now the point is to add a crucial dimension to the picture of heart-shaping. The good overwhelmings in our heart's core community, and in its giving and receiving hospitality, can go terribly wrong. It is precisely the best dynamics that have most potential for catastrophic distortion – 'the corruption of the best is the worst'. The wounds that most cruelly disfigure the heart are given and received between lovers, husbands and wives, parents and children, friends, long-term colleagues and partners – any relationship where deep trust and loyalty create potentially tragic vulnerability.

So the good and the bad overwhelmings are inseparable. We all know in ourselves the urge to avoid the bad by not risking the good. Why get married, when the agonies of divorce are all around us? Why have children, when it is clear that every parent who really cares pays a huge cost? Why trust beyond what is absolutely necessary, when everyone has stories of being let down? Can we even trust ourselves not to let others down under pressure?

It is a terrible dilemma. Do we try to resist being overwhelmed, and so close ourselves to life and love? Or do we commit ourselves in trust to child, spouse, friend, partner, group or cause, in the practical certainty of having to suffer a lot? Few of us resolve that dilemma by simply choosing one side of it. We work out all sorts of compromises and ways of staying relatively invulnerable while yet being committed. Our defences and securities vary according to our personality type, our experiences, and our little and large decisions over the years. But underlying them all is the fact of agonized fragility. Just facing this truth of our own fragility is a major step in the formation of a heart. How many divorces are due to one or both partners not being realistic about their own and the other's fallibility and vulnerability?

This vulnerability and the aching anxiety it brings makes us long for relief, security and comfort. How much damage is done to relationships by the unrealistic expectation of comfort? If 'what I feel comfortable with' is the standard for judging how a marriage or other relationship is going, it is almost bound to fail. This is because 'comfort' is a measure that cannot cope with being overwhelmed – in good ways or in bad. Yet it is, either openly or hiddenly, the main criterion for a great many expectations and decisions.

Addiction to comfort and security turns a heart in on itself. Its core community is policed very carefully. Threats to comfort are dealt with severely, often by creating no-go areas where fences can be built around those with most capacity for disruption. Previous and expected wounds justify a tight security policy. This applies even more at the frontiers across which the heart's hospitality can happen. The unpredictability of strangers makes the heart uncomfortable, and appeals in the faces and voices of others are better ignored or deflected.

So wounds and the fear of wounds can shape a heart turned in on itself which desires comfort and security. We recognize the hard heart, the cold heart, the closed heart, the paralysed heart, even the dead heart. But the same wounds can also help to transform a heart. Just as love can 'shift the boundaries of our being', so suffering can open us to dimensions of life that were unimaginable before. It is as if our heart is painfully excavated by suffering, its capacity expanded. The hurts can teach sensitivity and sympathy. We recognize in some people a heart that is beyond naïvety, that has 'been through it', but still trusts, welcomes and risks.

THE OVERWHELMED HEART

So what makes the difference? Why does one heart harden and close and another risk love and hospitality? We have no overview of hearts, and who can judge another? But we each need to gather whatever wisdom we can about this, because both possibilities are there daily for each of us. That wisdom comes most powerfully in testimonies. Contemporary literature is full of testimonies to hearts that have closed, despaired, been distorted or died. But there is also testimony to the other possibility.

O'Siadhail's 'Out of the Blue' is one example. It points to many of the classic marks of those who have had their hearts transformed. 'Nothing can explain this adventure' – there is no formula for it. It is risky, 'a blind date where foolish love consented in advance'. It is experienced as an astonishing gift: 'Should I dare to be so lucky? Is it a dream?' And it leaves us overwhelmed, 'beyond our fathom'. The secret is that amazing 'trip of surprises': 'this love re-invades us'.

But how does this relate to wounds? O'Siadhail tries to describe this too. In 'The Other Voice' he imagines the woman of 'Out of the Blue' speaking, addressing him as that man who had been humiliated as a schoolboy and whose wounds wore many faces, including despair and mockery:

You came lean and taut, a barrage of innocence.
I remember a bluster of haughtiness hiding a boy
still dazed with childhood hurts, a man tense
with desire; slowly I thawed and rocked you in joy.
You mocked our speck of being; I showed instead
of dust a galaxy whirling in the sunbeam's eye;
you cried at the size of eternity, I hushed and said

eons count as kisses under a lover's sky.
No half-measures then. I have made this island
of life a kingdom. Have I stinted your ease
or pleasure? No, how could a woman understand
that men still talk of freedom to go as they please?
My love is your freedom. Do or die or downfall,
it's all or nothing and I have chosen all.[5]

Is love like that the key to the cosmos? That is the daring sugges-
tion of the sonnet. The yearning to be 'rocked in joy' can be seen
as infantile, a longing to return to the cradle. Is it just false projec-
tion to see the universe not as indifferent to our 'speck of being'
but in terms of 'kisses under a lover's sky'?

Here is one of the most basic alternatives anyone can face. Some
believe the universe to be a brute fact ruled by chance. The most
radical alternative belief is that it is created by love for love and it
(together with ourselves) is in fact being loved now. This is a
stupendous vision: the cosmos is a place where things can go
terribly wrong, where there can be multiple bad as well as good
overwhelmings, but yet the most basic truth about it is that it is
loved and 'rocked in joy'.

What could possibly convince us one way or the other? The
sort of love O'Siadhail describes is a sign of the possibility that
love is the ultimate reality. It is of course easy to say that not
everyone experiences that. But the truth of 'The Other Voice' and
'Out of the Blue' is not that only if we have similar experiences are
we likely to be convinced. O'Siadhail is reaching towards something universal. As has often been seen, poetry strikes at the
universal all the more effectively because it strikes at it through
particular experiences. In a choice between regarding the universe
as brute fact or as created by and for love there can be no

neutrality. No one on earth has an 'objective' standpoint: that would require being able to stand outside it all in some way. For all the importance of being as intelligent as possible about our beliefs (that is what my own academic job is about), it is hard to imagine any ultimately convincing argument one way or the other. There are huge issues here, but let me go straight to what I see as the crucial one: whose testimony do we trust?

O'Siadhail is giving testimony to love. He knows that reality is such that we can have no certainty about this most important matter. It is an adventure which 'nothing can explain', and we proceed 'by hunch and guesswork'. He also knows that an inescapable part of it is wholehearted trust – 'No half-measures then'. This is something that is either overwhelming or it is nothing:

> My love is your freedom. Do or die or downfall,
> it's all or nothing and I have chosen all.

So he gives testimony and faces each reader with the possibility of trusting or not trusting him. The decision is intensely practical when we have the possibility of loving or receiving love. Is it worth the risk? Do we 'choose all'? Do we, like him, go on a 'blind date where foolish love consented in advance'? And, by pushing further and making it an issue of the way the cosmos is, his testimony reaches beyond falling in love or making friends. The stake now is whether, whatever the outcome in particular experiences of love, that 'lover's sky' says that we are always, unfailingly loved.

The Christian Gospel is this sort of truth. It is a testimony that is at heart very simple. It can be summed up in the words of those poems. It says God is committed to creation in words like those:

My love is your freedom. Do or die or downfall,
   it's all or nothing and I have chosen all.

It also says that the 'all' God chooses is utter loving involvement
for worse and for better, expressed decisively in Jesus Christ. And
it says that this makes possible the daily reality of 'Out of the
Blue':

Gratuitous, beyond our fathom, both binding and freeing,
   this love re-invades us, shifts the boundaries of our being.[6]

The final, crucial question of this chapter is how trusting this
testimony as reality shifts our boundaries and shapes our hearts.

BEING SHAPED THROUGH BEING OVERWHELMED

Jesus Christ is an embodiment of multiple overwhelming. He was
immersed in the River Jordan at his baptism, and then driven by
the Spirit into the wilderness to be tempted. He announced the
Kingdom of God as something worth everything else, a pearl
beyond price, a welcome beyond anything we could deserve, a
feast beyond our wildest desires. At the climax of his life he
agonized in prayer in Gethsemane, he was betrayed, deserted,
tortured and crucified, and he died crying 'My God! My God!
Why have you forsaken me?' (Mark 15:34)

Then came the resurrection, the most disorienting and transformative overwhelming of all. The testimonies to it are full of
stuttering amazement and confusion: 'And they went out and fled
from the tomb; for trembling and astonishment had come upon
them; and they said nothing to any one, for they were afraid'

(Mark 16:8). 'And when they saw him they worshipped him; but some doubted' (Matthew 28:17). 'But they were startled and frightened, and supposed they saw a spirit ... They still disbelieved for joy, and wondered ...' (Luke 24:37, 41)

Christian faith is about this person being central to the community of our heart. There he establishes a new core and also transforms our boundaries. The most daring prayer I know is about the transformation of boundaries that comes with Jesus Christ inhabiting our hearts:

> I kneel in prayer ... that through faith Christ may dwell in your hearts in love. With deep roots and firm foundations may you, in company with all God's people, be strong to grasp what is the breadth and length and height and depth of Christ's love, and to know it, though it is beyond knowledge. So may you be filled with the very fullness of God ... (Ephesians 3:14, 17–19, REB)

One of the most powerful expressions of this is by Paul in his Second Letter to the Corinthians. He speaks first of Christian transformation in terms of facing Jesus Christ:

> And we all, with unveiled face, beholding [or reflecting] the glory of the Lord, are being transformed into his likeness from one degree of glory to another; for this comes from the Lord who is the Spirit. (2 Corinthians 3:18)

Then he sums up his whole Gospel ('this treasure') as having the face of Christ shining in our hearts:

> For it is the God who said, 'Light will shine out of darkness,' who has shone in our hearts to give the light of the knowledge of the glory of God in the face of Christ. (2 Corinthians 4:6)

21

There overwhelming darkness is met by the light and glory of God. The form this takes in our hearts is the face of Christ. All that goes on in our hearts is before this face. Jesus Christ is the focus of our core community. That is the meaning of his being Lord, friend, mother, brother, host, guest, and more.

We could imagine having someone else as the focus of our life who would narrow our attention and limit our concerns. But to concentrate on the face of Jesus Christ is to find our boundaries shifting and expanding as we slowly 'grasp what is the breadth and length and height and depth of Christ's love'. This is someone whose hospitality is universal – face by face by face. To be before his face is to find that he is looking with love on all sorts of unexpected. marginalized or to us disagreeable people, as well as on us. Wherever he is he brings them as part of his community. So we find our heart is overwhelmed in new ways by those to whom his gaze, words and actions direct us. Even more broadly, as the mention of light in darkness underlines, all creation is embraced in this love, and we are invited to look with delight and responsibility on 'the face of the earth'.

This is a recipe for continual overwhelming. It is no accident that the initial explosion of new life after the resurrection of Jesus was in the form of wind and fire at Pentecost as the Holy Spirit was poured out. The Spirit is expressed in the elemental symbols of overwhelming: wind, fire, water, light, power. It is also the speech-giving Spirit, reversing Babel. It inspires prayer, singing, prophecy, teaching and testimony, and floods the world with good news. The Spirit is the self-distribution of the abundance of God, shaping each community and person differently. The Spirit inspires in us what the early Church called a 'sober intoxication'.

What is the way into all this? In the story of Pentecost, after his initial address to the crowd in Jerusalem, Peter is asked: 'What shall we do?' He replies:

> Repent, and be baptized every one of you in the name of Jesus Christ for the forgiveness of your sins; and you will receive the gift of the Holy Spirit. (Acts 2:38)

Baptism is the clearest Christian testimony to the fundamental and inescapable reality of being overwhelmed. It is the basic event of Christian identity. Those of us who are baptized have taken on an identity shaped by the overwhelmings of creation, death, resurrection and the Holy Spirit. We have also entered a community that spans the generations and relates us to many who have died, as well as to perhaps two billion people alive today who are identified as Christians. This is being overwhelmed by people; but it does not stop with the Christian community because Jesus Christ faces in love the four billion or so others too.

As we live before his face we find ourselves constantly re-invaded by love; as we follow his gaze we find our boundaries constantly shifting. This is the dynamic of being shaped by being overwhelmed.

TWO

VOCATIONS AND COMPULSIONS – LIFE-SHAPING DESIRES

What is a desire? It may be just a wish, but it may also dominate the life of a person or group. Such dominating desires are life-shaping. Desires are a common form of multiple overwhelming, and sorting them out is a lifetime's task. A helpful exercise is to ask ourselves what our main life-shaping desires are. What do we most want to do and be? What are the priorities we feel most deeply about?

Even if we can answer those questions, there are further complications. What we actually desire may be very different from what we think we ought to desire. We may long to have a certain desire, such as to love truth or God, but we may know that it is in fact little stronger than a wish in our lives, whereas other desires, which we would prefer not to have, grip us with compulsive force.

COMPULSIVE DESIRES

Almost any aspect of our life can give rise to overpowering desires. Eating, drinking, health, exercise, physical appearance, sport, sex, drugs: those are just a few of the areas directly to do with our bodies which can give rise to compulsions and addictions that fundamentally affect our whole lives. Similarly powerful compulsions can get hold of us in relation to our work, family, religion, money, the arts, social or political causes, entertainment, the life of the mind, psychotherapy, computers, and so on. None of these is bad in itself, but we all know what it feels like to be gripped by a desire in such a way that it takes us over until, against our better judgement, we start organizing our life around it.

Our economy and culture are like a machine manufacturing and orchestrating the desires of millions of people. The most obvious way this happens is through the entertainment industry, advertising and mass democratic politics. Our whole civilization would collapse if people started desiring in very different ways. Therefore massive forces are focused on making sure that that does not happen. These are the forces behind the compulsions, and it is difficult and sometimes dangerous to resist them.

What can anyone do in this turbulent whirlpool of desires, where many of the 'options' seem to be between desires that consume us, distract us, addict us, or otherwise manipulate us? The dynamics of desire are often treacherous. We can be attracted on to ground that, as soon as we commit our weight to it, proves to be a bog we cannot get ourselves out of.

Yet if we do not risk following our desires we risk not really living. All the best things in life are also the objects of desire: love, joy, justice, health, truth, goodness, beauty. To satisfy our desire for them, even in part, makes life and the dangers of desiring worthwhile. This brings us back to the central theme of this book: how to shape a life in the midst of good and bad overwhelmings – in this case the good and bad compulsions of desire.

EDUCATING FOR EXCESS

We are shaped by desires long before we become conscious of them or feel that we have any say in them. From the womb we are overwhelmed by them, and the dominating task of parents of a new baby is coping with its basic needs and desires. So our family is the main nursery of our desires. Every parent knows the demands not only of understanding and satisfying the desires of children at different stages (often more than one age simultaneously), but also of praising their desires, discouraging them, redirecting them, delaying their gratification and, at times, trying to plant new desires.

This universal process makes very clear one of the truths about desires which cannot be repeated too often: desires are not just 'given', they are not simply 'natural'. They require careful, wise attention, understanding and education. This does not mean that powerful desires are controllable or manageable in some manipulative way. That too is something parents quickly learn – or, if they do not, they and their children run the risk of short- and long-term disasters. It is just because desires are so uncontrollable that wisdom is all the more necessary. The height of wisdom may even be to discern when it is right for a particular desire to overwhelm us. In other words, we may need to be wary of the desire simply to control desires.

Families are not the only nurseries of desire. As mentioned above, our society is full of forces aiming to nurture and develop desires. They inundate us with images and options, and they compete for our attention, support and money. Immense intelligence and sophistication go into this, backed by huge resources of money and power. There is deep dissatisfaction with the dynamics of desire that these forces foster. We usually, however, as individuals, as families, and even as larger groups, feel power-less to affect the wider dynamics.

Faced with this situation, sensible people are usually attracted by some form of damage limitation which at its best aims for 'balance'. We attempt to discriminate among the forces that nurture desires, we build dams against the worst, we divert others, and we try to keep acceptable desires in balance. 'Nothing too much' is the maxim, and there is a long wisdom tradition devoted to 'the golden mean' – that balance to be found between extremes when desires are properly controlled.

Variations on that sensible solution are found in any family or community which continues to thrive. But it is not enough. The common sense of 'balance' by itself is simply not able to cope with the sheer vitality and effervescence of desires that knock so many of us off balance. People usually do not become addicted to money, food, drugs, drink or pornography for lack of such common sense. It is as if we sense, even in our worst excesses, that somehow we are made for excess. There must be best excesses too! So a balance that is constantly setting limits and never goes wholeheartedly with the flow of any desire is unable to contain the desiring energies of people. We yearn for more.

Fortunately, the sort of balance I have described is not the only sort. There is also a balancing which is dynamic and always on the point of overbalancing as it moves. It is like a bicycle being ridden, or an aeroplane in flight: if they stop, they crash. It is a picture of desires which are being shaped by one overwhelming desire. Such a great desire is the movement that integrates and balances all the others. We never feel in control of it. It constantly over-whelms us with demands and new possibilities. But take it away and we crash, our life seems dead – or we become victims of some lesser compulsion which fills the vacuum.

If desires are learnt and require nurturing in communities, and if families are not able to cope by themselves, then the most urgent question is where we find nurseries of such great, life-shaping desires. In fact we find them all around us: some schools; communities of artists; groups, movements and traditions of many sorts. But the largest and most experienced nurseries of desire are undoubtedly the religious traditions. They are acutely aware of the power of desire for better or for worse, and have devoted centuries of experiment to working out wisdoms of desire. I will explore what Christian wisdom is on this matter. It has a great deal in common with some other traditions, and also some decisive differences, but in this book my aim is not so much to compare and contrast as to outline one shape of living.

DESIRED BY GOD

There are two great simple Christian truths about desiring. The first is that God desires us.

This is perhaps the hardest truth of any to grasp. Do we wake up every morning amazed that we are loved by God, aware that this is the ultimate in delight, dignity and self-worth? Do we allow our day to be shaped by God's desire to relate to us? Are we ready to be stretched in our hearts, minds, imaginations, actions and sufferings in order to do justice to this glorious God? Do we habitually see ourselves, other people and creation in the light of God's desire for us all to flourish? Do we simply long to enjoy God?

I remember asking a friend, who had been a Roman Catholic priest for twenty years, what was the most common problem he met in hearing confession. He answered without hesitation:

'God'. He said that very few of those he hears in confession really behave as if God is a God of love, forgiveness, gentleness and compassion. Their biggest barrier is a God seen as being very different from the God of Jesus Christ, who welcomes home the Prodigal Son with an embrace and a party. They cannot believe that God values them, delights in them, suffers for them, is interested in the detail of their lives, has a way through their particular sins and difficulties, and has a calling for them.

The odd thing is that, even though we find it almost impossible to accept from God, our deepest desire is to be desired, and to be able to respond. St Augustine said to God in his *Confessions*: 'You have made us for yourself and our hearts are restless till they rest in you.' Those *Confessions* are a classic on the subject of desire – Augustine had a turbulent, passionate life, his mind and heart exploring in all directions before he eventually recognized the truth in that statement. In the course of his life he was to return time and again to the theme of desire. His basic point is that, if we get the desire for God right, everything else follows. The daring principle he offers is: 'Love God and do what you like.' This is because really to love God is what harmonizes all other desires. That is the great, life-shaping desire that keeps us in the sort of dynamic spiritual balance that is constantly being rightly overwhelmed by God's desire for us and ours for God.

So there is no doubt what our great, life-shaping desire should be. Jesus echoed his Jewish tradition when he said that the first and great commandment is to love God with all our heart, soul, mind and strength. That is the only wise, long-term, utterly fulfilling desire. But it is only so because of the more fundamental truth that God loves and desires us.

I love the mutuality of the psalmist and God:

You have said, 'Seek my face'.
My heart says to you,
'Your face, Lord, do I seek.' (Psalm 27:8)

That seeking of the face of God is the great passion of Jews and Christians. The 'vision of God' has been at the heart of their yearnings century after century. But it is easy to forget the mutuality. It is not as if God is distant and invites us on a long expedition to find him. It is rather the other way round. God is, as Augustine said, closer and more intimate to us than we are to ourselves. It is we who are distracted, who miss the 'one thing necessary' and pursue all sorts of other desires. We are found long before we find. When we begin to find God we realize that God has already found us. The desire is in fact overwhelmingly on God's side, as the experience of my priest friend confirms.

So what can open us up to responding to God's desire for us? Everyone's story is different, and we should never suppose we really know anyone else's – or even our own story, since we are deeply mysterious to ourselves, and only God really knows us. There are endlessly varied ways in which people awake to God's love for them. Most come to it through family, friends and worshipping communities. But almost any means can be an occasion for the conversion to begin, including what has been called 'the providence of the right book at the right time'. Classically it is ascribed to 'grace', and that gentle word helps us to remember what sort of God we are dealing with: one who would never coerce us, and is humble enough repeatedly to invite, appeal and even plead with us. We are never in a position to have an overview of what is happening in the dramas of grace in our own lives or the lives of others, but our main calling is clear: to let ourselves be desired and loved.

DESIRING WHAT GOD DESIRES

The second great Christian truth about desiring is that we are invited to desire what God desires.

In desiring what God desires we find the long-term shape of our life. It is like other relationships of love. The face-to-face, intimate dimension is vital, but to be healthy it needs to go with activities in which we are side by side, jointly engaged in common enterprises, committed to similar aims. In marriage the most common focus for this is children, in which the desires of the parents come together, and the demands and joys of the family continually draw them beyond their own face-to-face mutuality. God too desires that families be built up, that work be done, and that other worthwhile activities happen.

Clearly the first thing God desires is that we respond with our desire for him. In practice we often move in the direction of desiring God by trying to live in accordance with what we think are his other desires. The first thing in importance is not always the first thing in our experience. The taste for God often grows by living, almost without realizing it, in ways that please him. Habits of respect for other people, faithfully fulfilling our responsibilities, going to church, having compassion for the marginalized or suffering, praying regularly according to some pattern, reading the Bible – these and many other practices come into the category of Christian common sense. It is taken for granted that God desires them. The last thing we should do is to wait to begin doing them until we have certain feelings or experiences of God. It is much more likely that feelings will follow the practices.

God's desires for us are in broad outline very clear. They are to do with love, faith, hope, worship, following Jesus Christ, service, seeking wisdom, doing justice, honesty, and such like. The

31

problem is that they seem overwhelming: just reading the Sermon on the Mount can be a very discouraging experience, let alone all the rest of the Bible. It is not only the abundance of biblical testimony to what God desires that causes the problem; Christian history gives hundreds of models of Christian living, and the churches around the world today are also full of recipes. Then there is all the wisdom of other traditions, philosophies and religions. Part of the Christian vocation is to cope with this abundance, both as communities and as individuals. It has to be constantly engaged with afresh by each person and community. The next chapter tackles the question of the ability to please God in practice while confronting overwhelming demands and multiple possibilities. But the shaping of our desires is more fundamental even than that. So we first need to allow our desires to be educated by learning from the vocation of Jesus Christ, from the vocation of the worshipping community, and from the accumulated wisdom of those who have attempted to shape their own lives according to God's desires.

JESUS CHRIST – DESIRE AND COMPULSION

It is remarkable that almost nothing is told of the first thirty years of Jesus's life after his early months. After a few childhood incidents he bursts on the scene at the River Jordan, asking to be baptized by John the Baptist. Those 'hidden years' are worth thinking about. Obviously they were not irrelevant to his few years in the public eye. They must have included all sorts of things that fed into his ministry. At the very least we can imagine things which, if he had done them, would have undermined his ministry before it began. His appreciation of God in the details of life ('the

32

hairs of your head are numbered', 'every careless word ...') could not exclude himself. The same is true of us. Nothing is irrelevant to our vocation. We may have what feel like 'hidden years', spent on apparently disconnected activities and 'details' without any great sense of integrating purpose, only to find later that the quality of those details has been crucial for fulfilling a life's work.

We do not know how Jesus's desires were educated – the massive Christian interest in Mary his mother is relevant here. But the basic truth of Christian desiring is clear right at the start of his public life. At Jesus's baptism he hears 'a voice from heaven, "You are my beloved Son; in you I delight"' (Luke 3:22). Jesus is desired by God. He is affirmed by God as radically as possible. He has a parallel 'peak experience' of God's affirmation at a later turning-point. In his transfiguration, the divine voice again comes: 'This is my Son, my Chosen; listen to him!' (Luke 9:35). So he is loved, delighted in, chosen by God. That is at the root of his identity.

The other key element in Jesus's baptism is that the Holy Spirit comes upon him. John's gospel says that Jesus has the Spirit 'without measure' (John 3:34). It is an abundance which overflows in wisdom, teaching with authority, healings, exorcisms, prayer, visions, prophecy, and above all a clarity about his mission. Jesus was a Spirit-filled person in the charismatic stream of the Judaism of his time, and there are parallels to much of what he did and said. But his primary distinctiveness is how, in the Spirit, he worked out his vocation and fulfilled it – his doing what God desired.

A prime example of this comes immediately after his baptism. Jesus, 'full of the Holy Spirit', is tempted in the wilderness, and all three temptations are aimed at his identity as Son of God and the vocation which goes with that (Luke 4:1–13). Overwhelmed by hunger after forty days of fasting, his desire for food is set against his desire to be Son of God in God's way. He is next given a glimpse of absolute power over all the kingdoms of the world, if only he will worship the devil. Finally, he is tempted by the prospect of a spectacular short cut to fame and divine confirmation by throwing himself from the parapet of the Temple and trusting God to save him.

Here are some of the strongest human desires: for physical satisfaction and comfort, for power and influence, for reputation and success without the cost that gives them substance. In Jesus's temptations we find them in conflict with the desire to be true to God. We also find a basic principle for resisting temptation and allowing life to be shaped by what God desires: obedience. In each temptation Jesus quotes and obeys scripture: 'Man is not to live on bread alone'; 'You shall do homage to the Lord your God and worship him alone'; 'You are not to put the Lord your God to the test.'

What is obedience? It is very easily misunderstood. In our culture the word has gone out of fashion, partly because it has been abused by authoritarians who want to impose blind obedience. Partly, too, it has been seen as a violation of people's freedom, integrity and maturity. But no society can do without it, and we don't have to look far to see new names being used for good and valid forms of obedience. In our culture at present the most popular terms are accountability and responsibility. They describe how we ask that people keep to certain principles, rules and guidelines and be answerable to appropriate authorities, whether a parent, an electorate, a company, a superior, a 'charter', or a professional organization. Already we can see signs that these terms too are getting a bad name, but if they are discarded they will have to be replaced – and maybe obedience will come back into fashion.

Jesus in the wilderness is being accountable to God and the word of God, and is taking responsibility for his life and mission. The crucial thing for his vocation, and for ours, is to whom he is accountable and before whom he is responsible: the God who loves and delights in him. His obedience is in recognizing that he himself is God's desire and that everything else in his life should be in tune with the desires of God. It is inconceivable for Jesus that, whatever the hardships, God would lead him on a way that is not right, good and ultimately the fulfilment of his deepest and truest desires. We need to remember that our vocation is not alien to our creation: it is the fulfilment of what we have been created for.

Does this violate our freedom? But does love violate our freedom? In the previous chapter each of Micheal O'Siadhail's love poems saw the answer to this. In 'The Other Voice' the questions have a note of the incredulity at how love can be so mistrusted and misunderstood:

Have I stinted your ease
or pleasure? No, how could a woman understand
that men still talk of freedom to go as they please?
My love is your freedom.[1]

In 'Out of the Blue' the apparent paradox of the compulsion of love is summed up in a line. Love is

Gratuitous, beyond our fathom, both binding and freeing.

Looking at Jesus we have that impression of him being both free and bound in love for God. There is a deep sense of compulsion about his mission: 'I am sent...'; 'It is necessary...';

'I must...'; 'Not my will but yours be done.' But it is a sense of 'right compulsion', of a hard but good task to be done. There is no sense that his freedom need be in competition with God's will.

So wise obedience is the committed, focused and therefore 'binding' freedom to do what is right. It is the combination of accountability and responsibility which we find in our most important relationships – with spouses, our own children, close friends, or collaborators in an urgent task. But, given the usual confused and conflictual state of our desires, the compulsions that get hold of us are by no means always right ones. Strong forces in ourselves and our society conspire to make sure we stay in the power of wrong compulsions. Often the strongest compulsions of all are apparently non-coercive ones which only show themselves when they are challenged, such as an addiction to comfort, security, status or success.

Jesus embodies liberating obedience to what is right, and resistance to the many temptations to go another way. One of the meanings of 'Jesus is Lord' is, therefore, that he embodies the right compulsion of love and is to be obeyed. A central truth of human nature is that we have no choice over whether we have compulsive desires. But will they be in accordance with the desires of God? In the midst of the chaos of compulsions, wise obedience creates a shape of living.

THE TRANSFORMING IMAGINATION

Jesus did not just quote scripture and tell people to obey it. In fact he did so rarely, and even then often gave it an unexpected twist. He realized that the secret of desiring something lies more in the imagination than the will. So he constantly worked on people's imaginations. He was a master of the dramatic action and the apt reply. He did and said eminently memorable things that gripped hearts and minds. In all this he had one overriding aim. He stated it at the very beginning of his ministry after his temptations: 'The time has arrived; the kingdom of God is upon you. Repent, and believe the good news' (Mark 1:15).

That word 'repent' means a transformation of mind and heart. The way Jesus went about it showed how critical the imagination is in this. The Kingdom of God was to be the great desire, shaping all others. He said: 'Seek first the kingdom of God and his right-eousness [or justice], and everything else shall be added to you' (Matthew 6:33). That is an amazing promise. It is the principle of the balance in movement that is single-minded about its great desire. If we really put the desires of God first everything else falls into place – though maybe in surprising ways.

How did Jesus convert imaginations to desire the Kingdom of God? His main way was by telling parables. Here is one of the shortest:

> The kingdom of heaven is like treasure lying buried in a field.
> The man who found it, buried it again; and for sheer joy he went
> and sold everything he had, and bought that field. (Matthew
> 13:44)

That has most of the main elements in Christian calling: finding something overwhelmingly valuable; feeling compelled and delighted at the same time; and risking an overwhelming commit-ment in response.

It sounds as if the treasure was found by accident; the next little parable is about finding a specially beautiful pearl and selling everything for it, but this time the finder is an expert who is looking for pearls. He was energetically seeking his heart's desire.

Another set of parables turns the tables. They are about being found. We imagine ourselves as a lost sheep found by its shepherd, as a lost coin found by a woman, and as the Prodigal Son lost by his father (Luke 15). In each case the final emphasis is on celebration: 'Rejoice with me!' (v.6); 'Rejoice with me!' (v.9); 'Let us have a feast!' (v.23).

I remember once at a theological conference, in the middle of a complicated discussion of the Kingdom of God, a senior New Testament scholar stood up and said: 'The main thing the New Testament says is that the Kingdom of God is a party.' It is something to be desired and excited about. Jesus had all sorts of other things to say about it too, but there is no doubt what the basic message is: God, like the Prodigal's father, desires, loves and forgives us with such astonishing generosity that we find it very hard to imagine and take seriously.

Whether we are looking for it or not, God has a future for us that can fulfil our desires beyond our wildest dreams. This is a God of excess, of superabundance and overwhelming. Did God not create this vast universe, and all the complex forms of matter and life? Yet Jesus is also sure that God notes what happens to every sparrow, let alone us. Among the abundance, and through the details of our desiring, each of us is being shaped.

OPEN TO DEATH

Jesus was also a realist. He was quite clear that to speak and behave in line with the reality of this type of God meant that many people would not stand it. It threatened all sorts of vested interests to do with religion, money, family life, politics and status

38

(just read the Sermon on the Mount, Matthew chapters 5–7!). Most of the strongest human desires are bound up in those interests. Jesus taught and demonstrated an alternative which above all centred on desiring God and the Kingdom of God. The stakes were as high as could be, and he knew well that the ultimate stake is life itself. This meant facing death.

I have a friend, Nicholas Peter Harvey, who has himself faced up to death over many years and has also written about Jesus and death.[2] He writes about the Dutch Jewish woman, Etty Hillesum, who has left a diary and letters of the months in a transit camp before she was sent to Auschwitz, where she died. Her writings show her facing death and God together, and undergoing a remarkable transformation. She was liberated to love life, to help other people and to write vividly and movingly of the events around her. At the heart of her transformation was a continually renewed focusing on what really mattered in the face of death. She wrote in a letter:

> People here fritter their energy away on the thousand irksome details that grind us down every day; they lose themselves in detail and drown. That's why they get driven off course and find existence pointless. The few big things that matter in life are what we have to keep in mind; the rest can be quietly abandoned. And you can find those few big things anywhere, you have to keep rediscovering them in yourself so that you can be renewed. And in spite of everything you always end with the same conviction: life is good after all ... And that's what stays with me, even now, even when I'm about to be packed off to Poland with my whole family.[3]

The point Harvey makes is that we all, at some level, know we will die, but we repress our sense of death. It affects us in many indirect ways which sap life of its joy or let us lose ourselves in detail. When Etty Hillesum faced it, not stoically, anxiously or despairingly, but with confidence in a God of life, then she could live vibrantly in the face of death.

One of the deepest secrets of Jesus's vocation was that he had an unrepressed sense of death. He taught his disciples that there was no following the way of the Kingdom of God without being willing to stake their life on it: 'Anyone who wishes to be a follower of mine must deny himself and take up his cross and follow me' (Mark 8:34); 'Whoever seeks to gain his life will lose it, but whoever loses his life will preserve it' (Luke 17:33). A vocation which has not reckoned with death in this way is likely to develop without joy. It is a basic instance of overwhelming: abundance of life and immersion in death are inseparable. How can we hope to shape our lives wisely if we have not faced up to death and are willing to risk it? Only that can give us the realism, confidence and vibrancy to desire what really matters before God.

WORSHIP AS THE SHAPING OF DESIRE

What is the secret of the Psalms? Over thousands of years they have been at the heart of the worship of Jews and Christians. Perhaps no book has been more influential. The Psalms have given whole communities and traditions their public voice and have formed the private prayer of billions of people. They have drawn generation after generation into the great overwhelmings – by God, joy, suffering, anger, gratitude, fear, enemies, prosperity, hope, despair, trust, glory, humiliation, guilt, praise, blame, and much more.

They cry out from the depths of the worst that can happen:

Save me, O God! For the waters have come up to my neck.
I sink in deep mire, where there is no foothold;
I have come into deep waters, and the flood sweeps over me.
 (Psalm 69:1–2)

They also see all creation taken up into praise of God's encompassing glory:

Praise him, sun and moon, praise him, all you shining stars! ...
Mountains and all hills, fruit trees and all cedars!
Beasts and all cattle, creeping things and flying birds!
Kings of the earth and all peoples, princes and all rulers of the
 earth!
Young men and maidens together, old men and children!
Let them praise the name of the Lord, for his name alone is
 exalted;
his glory is above earth and heaven. (Psalm 148:3–13)

There is not only realism about passions, chaos, hatred, death and destruction – there is submersion in them, and bitter lament. The joy, praise and abundance of good things are not answers or 'solutions' to all that. It is a much more richly complex picture of multiple overwhelming which has only one sure orientation – to God.

The result is that the Psalms are an education in desire for God. A classic expression of desire shaped through the depths and the heights is Psalm 63:

O God, thou art my God, I seek thee, my soul thirsts for thee;
my flesh faints for thee, as in a dry and weary land where no
 water is.

So I have looked upon thee in the sanctuary, beholding thy
power and glory.

Because thy steadfast love is better than life, my lips will praise
thee.

So I will bless thee as long as I live; I will lift up my hands and
call on thy name.

My soul is feasted as with marrow and fat, and my mouth praises
thee with joyful lips,

when I think of thee upon my bed, and meditate on thee in the
watches of the night;

for thou hast been my help, and in the shadow of thy wings I
sing for joy.

My soul clings to thee; thy right hand upholds me.

But those who seek to destroy my life shall go down into the
depths of the earth;

they shall be given over to the power of the sword...

Desire for God is the dynamic of the whole of life, illuminating it, deepening involvement in it, and directing energies and hopes; but, beyond that, God's 'steadfast love is better than life'. So death is not the ultimate, it is relativized by God.

In the climax of Jesus's passion and death, as he desires above all to do God's will, there is a convergence of his crying out to God in forsakenness, his trust in God, and his sheer physical agony. The gospels describe him turning to Psalm 22:1, Psalm 31:5 and Psalm 69:21 to express each of these. This is more than just quotation: it shows a mind and heart saturated with the Psalms, so that in his extremity of suffering at the point of death, they are his spontaneous exclamation.

Luke's note of forgiveness from the cross, 'Father, forgive them; for they know not what they do' (Luke 23:34), leads even further when placed against the psalmist's usual attitude to enemies, as seen above in the last lines quoted from Psalm 63. Jesus as it were takes the cursing prophecy, 'Those who seek to destroy my life shall go down into the depths of the earth', and turns it into forgiveness and an exchange: he is the one who goes into the depths of the earth for others. He identifies not only with the 'innocent' psalmist but also with his 'guilty' enemies. This offering of himself is the ultimate worship, and it means that his death becomes the pivot of every Christian's vocation and worship. The classic expression of this is a vocation rooted in baptism, and worship rooted in the Eucharist, each of which unites the education of our desires with participation in the passion and death of Jesus Christ.

FAITHFUL DESIRING – PROMISES

'We made our covenants,' said O'Siadhail's lover in 'Out of the Blue'. Like the Church, marriage – that other great school of desire – has the wisdom of promising at its heart. Promising is an extraordinary phenomenon. A promise is utterly fragile, so easy to break; yet it can also generate bonds that last a lifetime, and endure ups and downs, terrible sufferings, even betrayal, torture or the threat of death. A relationship or group of any depth will, if it wants to last through the sufferings, joys, boredoms and distractions of life, draw on the language and practices of promise-keeping (even if the promises that bind them are never spoken): trust, loyalty, faithfulness, hope, patience, endurance, remembering. Promising is one of the main ways in which a shape of life is maintained through good and bad overwhelmings. It is the translation of desiring into faithfulness. As the marriage service puts it, we are committed 'in sickness, in health, for richer, for poorer, till death us do part'.

In Christian baptism (and confirmation) promises are vital too. But that is for each person one by one. The foundational promise between a community and God is called in the Bible 'the covenant'. Much of the Old Testament can be read as the story of the covenant between God and Israel, which was often compared to a marriage. 'Testament' means covenant, and Christians believe that Jesus Christ brought a 'New Testament', a new stage in the covenant relationship of the people of God. It is of the utmost importance that this should not be seen (as sometimes in Christian history) as undoing the covenant with Israel and the ongoing covenant in which Jews live today (Paul is very clear about this in Romans chapters 9–11). But the New Testament does invite other peoples into the covenant relationship, and has at its heart those new events of multiple overwhelming, Jesus's crucifixion and resurrection and the outpouring of the Holy Spirit at Pentecost. Jesus is himself seen as 'the Yes pronounced upon God's promises, every one of them' (2 Corinthians 1:20). Baptism is a promise of faithfulness to him – it includes, therefore, entering into the promises of the Old Testament too. It also includes entering into the joint promises made between the Church and God.

These promises between God and the Church are awesome on both sides. In the Methodist Church there is a special Covenant Service, usually repeated once a year, around New Year, in order to allow members to commit themselves afresh to this covenant. I was introduced to it when my colleague, Frances Young, and I were teaching in the Centre for Black and White Christian Partnership in Selly Oak Colleges, Birmingham. She led the service for the course and guests, a gathering that embraced about a dozen different denominations. I remember thinking: this, after the Eucharist, is the most moving Christian liturgy I know.

The final part of the Covenant Service opens with this strong statement of the meaning of the covenant. It could serve as a basic framework for all Christian vocations:

[*The People stand and the Minister says:*]
Beloved in Christ, let us again claim for ourselves this Covenant which God has made with his people, and take the yoke of Christ upon us.

To take his yoke means that we are content that he appoint us our place and our work, and that he himself be our reward.

Christ has many services to be done; some are easy, others are difficult; some bring honour, others bring reproach; some are suitable to our natural inclinations and material interests, others are contrary to both. In some we may please Christ and please ourselves, in others we cannot please Christ except by denying ourselves. Yet the power to do all these things is given in Christ, who strengthens us.

Therefore let us make this Covenant of God our own. Let us give ourselves anew to him, trusting in his promises and relying on his grace.

It then culminates, before Holy Communion, in the most radical 'binding and freeing' as each member renews his or her vocation.

[*The Minister says:*]
Lord God, Holy Father, since you have called us through Christ to share in this gracious Covenant, we take upon ourselves with joy the yoke of obedience, and, for love of you, engage ourselves to seek and do your perfect will.

We are no longer our own, but yours.
[*The people respond:*]
I am no longer my own but yours. Put me to what you will, rank me with whom you will; put me to doing, put me to suffering; let me be employed for you or laid aside for you, exalted for you or brought low for you; let me be full, let me be empty; let me have all things, let me have nothing; I freely and wholeheartedly yield all things to your pleasure and disposal. And now, glorious and blessed God, Father, Son and Holy Spirit, you are mine and I am yours. So be it. And the covenant now made on earth, let it be ratified in heaven. Amen.

To desire that is only conceivable if we are assured that God's 'pleasure and disposal' are utterly for our good and our joy, and that we really can trust in his promises and rely on endless grace and forgiveness. And having glimpsed this astonishing vocation, 'married' to the God of the universe, is it worth living or dying for anything less?

WHAT ABOUT MY VOCATION?

'What about my vocation?' is a question that each of us should ask. There are many misunderstandings of 'vocation'. For many people it means either something specifically religious, or else a career or job. Or it is sometimes narrowed down still further to mean just some careers, those such as nursing or teaching, which might be seen as helping professions. I am taking it much more broadly to mean the long-term shaping of our lives by desires that we 'own'. Fulfilling these desires can of course include jobs and other work (which are discussed in chapter 5), but also every other aspect of life. The shapes of vocations can be astonishingly varied, even within one life at its different stages.

One common picture of a vocation is of an early sense of 'calling', which is then more or less successfully followed out through a lifetime. The shape which that sort of vocation suggests is a moving line, or a journey towards a destination. But there are many other valid shapes.

The great contrasting image to the journey is that of home-making: a vocation to build up community, make friends, welcome strangers, cultivate a garden. If your vocation is more of the home-making variety it may seem rather static and lacking in the drama of a journey. So it can be a liberation to be told that you do not have to think of your life as travelling single-mindedly along one road. The same goes for churches and other communities and organizations, all of which, whether businesses or sports clubs or political parties, have vocations in my sense. Some are more journey-oriented, shaping history in certain ways and achieving the aims of 'mission statements'; others resist being described in straight lines, and seem dedicated to creating a certain sort of environment for living or just doing something for the pleasure of it.

Besides journeying and home-building as shapes of life, there are others. Given the complexity of any life it is probable that each of us will need to imagine our lives in many images, or will find at different stages that we need to identify with new ones. It is a helpful exercise to ask ourselves what shape seems to fit our basic conception of our life. A story with a clear plot? A piece of music with variations on the same basic theme? One instrument in an orchestra? An abstract painting in which there seem to be a bewildering confusion of lines, forms and colours? A text to which our words and actions are footnotes? An underground root plant which has developed odd configurations as it spreads in various directions? A tree which has some branches lopped off as it grows new ones and produces annual crops? Some animal or bird? A business enterprise? A cog in a wheel? A little finger in a body? A makeshift assemblage of bits and pieces which sometimes hangs together well but mostly does not?

We are overwhelmed with possibilities, but it is one of the most deeply exciting things that can happen to find ourselves gripped by a desire which starts shaping our life in particular ways. If it is a desire for the God of Jesus Christ and for the desires of that God, then there is an accumulation of wisdom to learn from as we find ourselves gripped more deeply. The earlier part of this chapter has summed up some of the elements of that wisdom, distilled over centuries. Our vocation will not flourish if we ignore those basics: recognizing how we are loved and desired by God, worshipping and loving God, following Jesus, loving other people, facing death, and being members of a covenant community. They are the foundation and framework; or, to change the image, they are the light to travel by. Even when we are completely confused by the state and direction of our own life they give us plenty to be getting on with.

But recognizing our own particular vocation is a further matter. We may have to get rid of previous ideas about what we are really suited for. We may have to go through several false starts, and experience disappointment and failure. I remember a teacher in a college of music, full of students ambitious for success in performance, talking about the special quality of music produced by those who knew failure. We may even have to face a life in which we do not achieve recognition or success in the eyes of other people, while still being faithful to what we believe we are called to. Our life may seem to us to be just one bit of obedient loving after another (and even more bits of forgiven disobedience), with no obvious shape. Or we may have the sort of responsibilities that are impossible to fulfil yet unavoidable: a great many worthwhile tasks are beyond anyone's capacity but yet must be attempted. Or we may have so many possibilities and gifts that we are spoilt for choice. What can help us as we try to discern and create our own very specific shape? I will mention just six guiding sayings that have been important for many, but these are meant as a stimulus to readers to add the wisdom they have learnt as they have tried to discern the right shape for life.

First, 'seek and you will find'. Confident seeking is the other side of the fact that we have already been found by God and called by God, whether we realize it or not. But beware: God tends to take us more seriously (and joyfully) than we take ourselves. As we timidly ask the big questions about the meaning and shape of our life we are likely to find answers beyond anything we imagined. It is common to reflect afterwards, when what (in retrospect) feels like a relatively manageable life has become multiply overwhelmed by God, that one had no idea what one was letting oneself in for.

Second, remember key events, periods, insights and turning-points of the past. It is easy simply to forget the signs of our vocation, or to fail to cultivate seeds which we were so delighted to be given.

Third, be alert for some key passages of the Bible to inhabit in a special way. Hans Urs von Balthasar has said that often a saint's whole life can be seen as living out just one verse of scripture. One rich verse or story can be essential to our vocation, as we come back to it year after year, and find further dimensions to it. The great words, verses and passages of scripture and the liturgy are like houses which, as we study, pray, suffer and love, are made habitable with our own furnishings, pictures, meals and children.

Fourth, be alert for role models, and testimonies to how other people have found and developed their vocations. It is not that any two are the same – that is part of the point. It can be immensely encouraging to appreciate the sheer variety of other vocations and life-shaping desires. But among them all it frequently happens that some one or two will grip us more deeply, and this is often important for our vocation. This personal relationship with particular 'saints' is a form of friendship (sometimes across many centuries), and like friendship it is rare to be able to have this in depth with more than a few.

Fifth, be looking for accompaniment in following a vocation. This might be in a group, or one-to-one with a pastor, 'soul friend' or spiritual director. It also might be in family life, which for many is a central part of their lives but often, sadly, not the place where vocations of parents and children are a central concern.

Sixth, the theme running through all the above sayings is: be alert! That is a constant biblical theme: watchfulness, wakefulness, seeing, hearing. It is above all alertness to a God of surprises who is more fully alive and active than we are. It is therefore common sense to see each day as full of the possibilities of engagement with God in discovering and inventing the shape of our life.

VOCATIONAL AUDIT

In 'Autumn Report'⁴ Micheal O'Siadhail in mid-life produces a statement of accounts on his life: 'I tender friends and shareholders an interim report ...' It speaks of the abundance of life:

Even in this fall, wholehearted life reverberates
some almighty gaiety, invites me to adore
the immense integrity; wines my veins until
I'm sure my frame will warp under such
exuberance. I've never felt so near the centre
of all that is.

He then reflects on following his vocation as a poet, with the constant new beginnings and his dominant desire,

the urge to utter. In this instant I'm Adam
the first to mouth, to feel the garden overflow
in word and rhythm.

The sheer grind of it, and the vulnerability to discouragement and despair are taken into account:

Yes, there were certain liabilities
to meet: mornings which would not wake, days
that moped and brooded on their failure until
shame, an unfed stomach, turned the acid fuel
to gnaw the lining. Dozing on, I recapped each collapse,
idly watched the digital clock matchstick
away my time, slip noiselessly into desperation.

But there are resources for coping even with that – the 'community of the heart' and even something more embracing:

Yet reaffirmed by woman's ardour, again allowed
untense, surrender afresh to laughter, I have
unjailed the self. Some all-embracing love

forgives my shortfall and I am glad to present
this reconciled account.

Then through all the overwhelmings and daily disciplines the
final notes are the worthwhileness of risking a vocation like this,
and the overflow of freedom that results:

Why hedge our bets
or play too cool? Detached we might miss
the passion to broaden the bore, deepen the joy.

The wind freshens, risks another leaf or two,
floats some unbidden debenture. Please give me
a few moments more, just to exult in this
last reflux of summer, luxuriate in its praise.
Then gambling on, I'll bless the breeze and go.

POWER, VIRTUE AND WISDOM – THE SHAPING OF CHARACTER

Why do we feel a shock of surprise and delight at real goodness? Generosity when resources are limited, courage when there is plenty to lose by it, patience beyond anything we deserve: these touch us to the core. And if, somehow, we occasionally do that sort of thing ourselves, we have a sense of being initiated into deep sources of life, energy and joy. Even more amazing than particular acts is the good person who does them frequently, year after year. We never know the full inside story of those years – and from the inside they often seem far from 'good'. But we occasionally glimpse the long-term shape of a life that has been faithful and generous in loving, and we stand in awe. Kierkegaard called this 'historical beauty', and recalled the faces of some old married couples after a lifetime together.

What is the secret of that beauty? We are aware of all sorts of 'explanations' of human behaviour, from genes and childhood experiences to economic circumstances and cultural conditioning. Yet we know people who seem to have all the advantages and who yet have not been able to sustain the joys and sufferings of love, or show that beauty. Likewise we know those who shine against a dark background of experiences and circumstances. Even more important, in our own case we realize that, however much we may blame the many factors that helped make us as we are, we still have our responsibility. No one, including ourselves, may be able to draw the line where our responsibility ends and beyond which we are purely victims, but for the sake of our moral health it is usually wise to assume more rather than less responsibility.

The long-term living out of responsibilities is my definition of the shaping of good character. It is a daily drama of virtues and vices, as our desires and compulsions pass over into patterns of behaviour. The stakes are as high as possible – lives spoilt or made radiant, hearts closed in fear or opened in hospitality, and the flourishing or not of marriages, families, businesses, institutions and nations. But the secret of really good character, which gives that shock of surprise and exhilaration, and which has the capacity to help energize the goodness of others, does not lie just in following good principles or doing our duty or any of the other formulas for goodness, though these have their place. It is beyond formulas, and clearly has to be a secret that is up to coping with the multiple overwhelmings of life. The secret is therefore itself likely to be overwhelming. This chapter is about the Christian way of being overwhelmed by goodness in joyful responsibility.

JOYFUL RESPONSIBILITY

Let us face at the start the main, shocking challenge. It is summed up by Jesus in the Sermon on the Mount: 'You, therefore, must be perfect, as your heavenly Father is perfect' (Matthew 5:48). That is an overwhelming demand. But its meaning may surprise us. It clearly depends on how God is perfect – but how is that? The Sermon on the Mount and the rest of Jesus's teaching and actions give more than enough clues.

God 'makes his sun rise on the evil and on the good, and sends rain on the just and on the unjust' (Matthew 5:45); God rewards what is done in secret; God forgives; God is to be trusted to take care of all our needs; God gives good things to those who ask him. God's greatest joy is in inviting everyone to a feast and laying the best before them. So God gives and forgives abundantly, and expects us to give and forgive abundantly: this is the great virtuous circle of joyful responsibility. The crucial thing is: God is utterly for us, but that is not at all in order to take away our responsibility. On the contrary, God is for us so that we can be wholeheartedly for God and for other people. God shares both joy and responsibility. And God always gives us more than enough to enable us to follow divine desires. Within all this, virtues are our habits of being for other people in ordinary life. They spring from hearts shaped as we have described in the previous two chapters: by Jesus Christ as the host of our 'community of the heart', and by God's desire for us and ours for God. The abundance of God means that the grace and energy to be virtuous are always available.

That is what Jesus taught, but who could receive it? Neither his enemies nor his followers. He offered everything and demanded everything. His practice of his own teaching led to his crucifixion. The cross is the culmination of his radical responsibility for others before God. His resurrection is the joy of someone who has taken full responsibility and can then inspire others. Pente-cost is that inspiration of joyful responsibility energizing a movement.

That, in brief, is the core of the good news which centres on the multiple overwhelming of crucifixion, resurrection and the Holy Spirit. It will be explored further later, especially in chapters 6 and 7. But what is its significance for the shaping of character? It means that virtues are the habits needed for a full life of joyful responsibility with and for others before God. It is no use thinking of living only a 'good enough' life when faced with this God. God wants nothing less than full responsibility and utter joy, and offers all that is needed for this. God gives all, and, as we fail, goes on forgiving all and giving more. God gives scandalously overwhelming and excessive love. Once we begin to see this, we see how our vices are all ways of being blind to love, avoiding it, rejecting it, or just being, in the full biblical sense, *fools* who miss the big, essential, many-splendoured thing. We also see why the supreme Christian virtue has always been love on the model of Jesus's words: 'Love one another as I have loved you.' That is the 'virtuous circle' of what Simone Weil calls 'new, marvellous, intoxicating goodness'.

POWER

But the obvious, normal reaction is still: impossible! ridiculous! That rightly draws us deeper into the cross and resurrection. If the message is just about a new example or ethical teaching or ideal then it is nice but useless. The vital matter is *power*. That makes the difference between our desire and its realization, between our intention and our action. Virtues are about real actions, reactions and interactions. What can shape them in line with Jesus's invitation to be perfect like God?

It is hard to over-emphasize the importance of power and the closely related realities of energy, strength, inspiration, will and authority. The life of Jesus was shot through with issues of power: temptations and conflicts about it, claims to it, use of it, misunderstandings of it and surrender of it. His death and resurrection released extraordinary power. But what sort?

Jesus's power is marked by taking complete responsibility on himself, and by trusting God completely at the same time. When he takes responsibility to the point of death, his Father answers his trust by raising him to new life and power. So Christian faith calls on God for this power embodied in the crucified and risen Jesus. The Holy Spirit is this power formed around the cross, and the root activity of all Christian life is calling out: 'Come, Holy Spirit!' The trust is that God will always give sufficient power for what he wants done: the loving that we are called to do this minute. The overwhelming of crucifixion, resurrection and Pentecost unite with the details of our life to produce the virtues and habits that shape our character.

But how is this related to every-day life? When I was a student a friend and I went to the ruins of the city of Ephesus in Turkey, near the Aegean coast. We camped (I think illegally) in the Temple of Vedius. So after all other tourists had gone we had a whole night and early morning to let the atmosphere have its effect. Each of us had taken Classics – ancient Greek and Latin and their civilizations – as his main subject, and had studied a little of the city's history. My friend was a German with a great interest in detail, and we tried to re-imagine the city and its life as we walked, with the metal on the heels of my shoes ringing on the marble paving. The ancient Greek and Roman world seemed to spring up around us. But for me, of all the images the strongest was of the Letter to the Ephesians being received and read in one of these little houses.

The small community that received the letter to the Christians in Ephesus was probably at the sensitive point of transition to the second generation of Christian faith. There is a sense in the letter of settling down for the long haul – strong concern for teaching the faith and for maturity in it; for the unity and ordering of the Church; for standing firm against all sorts of pressures; and for the behaviour of husbands and wives, parents and children, masters and slaves. Throughout it has a clear appreciation of how vital power is. Chapter 1 gives thanks for 'the immeasurable greatness of his power in us who believe, according to the working of his great might which he accomplished in Christ when he raised him from the dead...' (vv.19–20). The centre-point of the letter is the daring prayer which we looked at previously, in our own chapter 1. The prayer cries out for strength, might and power to love. It could well be the daily prayer of anyone who is attracted to travel the way of Christian virtue:

I bow my knees before the Father, from whom every family in heaven and on earth is named, that according to the riches of his glory he may grant you to be inwardly strengthened with might through his Spirit, and that Christ may dwell in your hearts through faith; that you, being rooted and grounded in love, may have power to comprehend with all the saints what is the breadth and length and height and depth, and to know the love of Christ which surpasses knowledge, that you may be filled with all the fulness of God.

Now to him who by the power at work within us is able to do far more abundantly than all that we ask or think, to him be glory in the church and in Christ Jesus to all generations, for ever and ever. Amen. (Ephesians 3:14–21)

In the remaining three chapters of the letter to the Ephesians the applications of that power are spelt out in detail for ordinary life. That life is described as a drama of virtues and vices, and it is worth listing them. The main virtues and good habits are humility, gentleness, patience, being tolerant of one another in love, maintaining unity and peace, speaking the truth in love, building a loving community, justice, holiness, honest work, helpful and encouraging speech, kindness, tender-heartedness, forgiveness, thanksgiving, obedience, honouring parents, and 'doing the will of God from the heart'. The main vices are deceit and lying, indecency, lust, nursing anger, stealing, using foul language, bitterness, slander and insults, malice, sexual immorality, greed, obscenity, disobedience, drunkenness, provoking children to anger, and threatening subordinates.

That could be a very discouraging list. Yet in the letter it is not, because the vital point is that there is actually the power available to cultivate the virtues and overcome the vices. It is realistically recognized that this is no smooth path. In fact the conclusion puts it in terms of a life and death fight requiring 'the whole armour of God' (6:11). But two things are clear and sum up the whole teaching of the Gospel on good and bad behaviour.

The first is that the key victory has been won: there is no doubt about who is Lord, and the fighting is, interestingly, seen as defensive only. Its aim is to 'withstand in the evil day, and having done all, to stand' (6:13). In other words, we already stand in the abundance of God's love, as the opening of the letter vividly described. The fight is to stay standing there, so we need to be equipped with truth, justice, the Gospel of peace, faith and God's word.

The second is that there is no doubt about the reality of the power and energy that are freely given. The culminating section begins: 'Finally, be strong in the Lord and in the strength of his might' (6:10). That is the imperative which underlies all the other commands about behaviour in ordinary life. But it is a strange sort of command – more like a reminder, when told to buy something, not to forget that there already is money in the bank.

We switch from Ephesus to Berlin in our own century. Dietrich Bonhoeffer is in prison for his resistance to the Nazis. He has been wrestling for over ten years with a deeply corrupt and corrupting regime. In one of his letters from prison he notes how often the New Testament tells us to 'be strong', and he concludes: 'Christ not only makes people "good"; he makes them strong, too.'[1]

THEREFORE ...

The open secret of practising virtues can now be clearly stated. It is seen in a pattern that occurs again and again in the New Testament. Directions about behaviour do not come first. Instead we find priority given to the overwhelming event of Jesus Christ. That is described vividly, and it often stretches our minds and imaginations. Then, often introduced by 'therefore ...', the focus switches to the behaviour which is the overflow of the power of that event.

Paul's letter to the Romans (which is probably the most influential letter in history) is the classic case. Near the beginning the Gospel is announced as 'the power of God for salvation to everyone who has faith' (1:16). The corruption of life by overwhelming vices is described:

> They were filled with all manner of wickedness, evil, covetousness, malice. Full of envy, murder, strife, deceit, malignity, they are gossips, slanderers, haters of God, insolent, haughty, boastful, inventors of evil, disobedient to parents, foolish, faithless, heartless, ruthless. (Romans 1:29–31)

Then comes the even more overwhelming event with which God meets all that:

But God shows his love for us in that while we were yet sinners Christ died for us. Since, therefore, we are now justified by his blood, ***how much more*** shall we be saved by him from the wrath of God. For if while we were enemies we were reconciled to God by the death of his Son, ***how much more***, now that we are reconciled, shall we be saved by his life. Not only so, but we also rejoice in God through our Lord Jesus Christ, through whom we have now received our reconciliation. (Romans 5:8–11)

That repeated 'how much more' is the crucial dynamic of transformation. It is repeated again and again in that chapter:'... how much more have the grace of God and the free gift in the grace of that one man Jesus Christ abounded for many' (5:15); '... how much more will those who receive the abundance of grace and the free gift of righteousness reign in life through the one man Jesus Christ' (5:17). Paul follows through the revolutionary meaning of this for one vital area after another – for sin and death, for the law, for being children of God, for the relations of Jews and Gentiles, for all creation, for everything that can ever happen to us:

Who shall separate us from the love of Christ? Shall tribulation, or distress, or persecution, or famine, or nakedness, or peril, or sword? ... No, in all these things we are more than conquerors through him who loved us. For I am sure that neither death, nor life, nor angels, nor principalities, nor things present, nor things to come, nor powers, nor height, nor depth, nor anything else in all creation, will be able to separate us from the love of God in Christ Jesus our Lord. (Romans 8:35–39)

Time and again Paul is overwhelmed with gratitude, amazement and praise:

Thanks be to God through Jesus Christ our Lord! (Romans 7:25)

God who is over all be blessed for ever. Amen. (Romans 9:5)

O the depth of the riches and wisdom and knowledge of God! How unsearchable are his judgements and how inscrutable his ways!

'For who has known the mind of the Lord,
   or who has been his counsellor?'
'Or who has given a gift to him
   that he might be repaid?'

For from him and through him and to him are all things. To him be glory for ever. Amen. (Romans 11:33–36)

It is immediately after this crescendo of awe at the mystery of God, generated by the good news of the event of Jesus Christ, that the great 'therefore ...' comes:

I appeal to you, therefore, brothers and sisters, by the mercies of God, to present your bodies as a living sacrifice, holy and acceptable to God, which is your spiritual worship. Do not be conformed to this world but be transformed by the renewing of your minds, that you may prove what is the will of God, what is good and acceptable and perfect. (Romans 12:1–2)

It has taken Paul eleven chapters to arrive at this point of teaching about behaviour. By this time, responding to the radical demand for transformation seems the least we can do to acknowledge this God and the love and power he shares. Virtues and other practices pour out – and each one could do with at least a chapter: humility, use of gifts, love, zeal in service, patience, constant prayer, sharing possessions, hospitality, blessing persecutors, rejoicing and weeping with those who rejoice and weep, living peacefully, refusing vengeance, doing good to enemies, overcoming evil with good, obedience to the political authorities, paying taxes, avoiding debt, obeying the commandments (summed up in 'You shall love your neighbour as yourself'), not judging fellow believers, the strong bearing with the weak, and much else. The tone is not at all one of commanding a heavy burden; it is more one of urgent encouragement and blessing on a demanding yet joyful journey:

> May the God of hope fill you with all joy and peace in believing, so that by the power of the Holy Spirit you may abound in hope. (Romans 15:13)

THE WAY TO VIRTUE

The strange truth is therefore that there is no direct way to goodness. We do not construct a good life by deciding to obey certain teachings, to follow our conscience, to stick to certain principles, to do our duty, to imitate good examples, or to develop virtues and good habits. There is something more fundamental than that sort of action. It is more like the 'active passivity' of letting ourselves be embraced, or letting ourselves be fed the food and drink that can energize us for virtue. I have been calling it 'being overwhelmed'. The way to goodness is through being immersed in that multiple 'how much more ...' of Romans 5. It leads straight to the secret of transformed living in Romans 6:

> We were buried therefore with him by baptism, so that as Christ was raised from the dead by the glory of the Father, we too might walk in newness of life. (Romans 6:4)

The willingness (or compulsion) to go this way of death, resurrection and new life is called 'faith' or 'trust' or 'belief' (the Greek word *pistis* means all three together). If it was not overwhelming it would not be the God-sized event that it is, and it could not cope with the reality of our world. It seems scandalous or unnecessary to anyone who thinks they can get on by themselves with a 'good enough' life. It seems unrealistic and too good to be true to anyone overwhelmed by problems, weaknesses or bad habits. It seems mythological and fantastic to anyone immersed in one (or a mixture) of the dominant worldviews and ideologies of the late modern West. It seems, to anyone who really appreciates it, like just what Paul says: being buried. But to that phrase is added 'with him' – with Jesus Christ, who is the one overwhelmed by death and now alive with the life of God. The deepest secret of Christian virtue is accompaniment by Jesus Christ in our overwhelmings. 'With him' means unfailing accompaniment through all our failures, and the unfailing energy of resurrection and Pentecost encouraging and redirecting us 'in newness of life'.

So the New Testament is extremely insistent on giving up vices and practising virtues, but it is even more insistent on doing both 'through Jesus Christ'. This seems an indirect, even foolish, way to solve the problem of sin and to get on with doing good. Many sensible, educated people find it scandalous, unrealistic, mythological or fantastic. But hundreds of millions of other sensible, educated people find that it is good news, and that it transforms their notions of scandal, reality, myth and fantasy. Vice and virtue have deep roots. They are nourished by hopes, fears and desires, by worldviews and ideas, by whatever feeds imaginations, hearts and minds. The Bible is deeply aware of these roots, and of the need for transformations in the whole 'ecosystem' of self, community and understanding, if virtues are to flourish. Ezekiel speaks of 'a new heart' and 'a new spirit' (36:26). Paul says that those 'in Christ' are 'a new creation' (2 Corinthians 5:17). In other words, only something so all-embracing is adequate. The 'good enough' is not good enough. The call is to something whole-hearted, a matter of life and death: a multiple overwhelming. As Paul says, it is the abundance of grace through Jesus Christ that gives the power of responding to the command: 'Be transformed!'

THE PASSION FOR WISDOM

That command actually says: 'Be transformed by the renewing of your minds, that you may prove what is the will of God, what is good, acceptable and perfect' (Romans 12:2). Think of the dimensions of that liberating instruction. It is fundamentally about seeking wisdom in all areas of behaviour. Where does this lead us?

Clearly it leads Paul as a Jew first of all to his Bible, which Christians came to call the Old Testament. There he found an abundance of wisdom about virtues and vices which he drew on for his ethical teaching in Romans and other letters. Within the overwhelming of the Holy Spirit he takes up the Old Testament passion for wisdom, which is above all about the shaping of behaviour before God, a passion that recognizes how crucial it is to shape our character and relationships in ways that distil what has been learnt by experience over many centuries.

But when scholars examine the Old Testament they find that its wisdom literature was not confined to Israel. Much of it was shared with neighbouring cultures and traditions. There are parallels in Egypt, Mesopotamia and further afield. In other words, the passion for wisdom about human behaviour was international and interreligious. It led people to reach out beyond their own traditions and draw on the best they could find elsewhere. Paul and other New Testament writers do the same. There is at present quite an industry among scholars showing the many parallels between the virtues and vices taught by the New Testament and those taught by Stoics, Cynics and various other schools of thought in the Roman Empire.

Down the centuries this continued in Christianity. Every period has had to work out responses to new questions and challenges. We tend to think we face unique moral dilemmas and crises, but human behaviour has always aroused controversy. Each generation has had its men and women who have improvised on their own and other traditions in order to help guide practice and education in new circumstances. This is the task of wisdom, drawing on everything relevant in order to open the way into the future before God. It is very rarely a matter of repeating the past exactly; it is also very rarely wise to ignore the past. There are therefore no rules from the past which can be obeyed mindlessly, and we are constantly having to take responsibility for acting without precedent. The responsibility of seeking wisdom is therefore essential if we are to try to live well. With power and virtue, this is the third, vital dimension in shaping character.

LISTS

Every culture has a repertoire of wise sayings to help guide behaviour. They distil what has been learnt from millennia of experience and reflection. I know someone who makes sure that he reads through the Book of Proverbs at least once a year, and always finds it freshly relevant. The riches of these condensations of insight emerge only slowly through a lifetime, as we ourselves move through different experiences and allow the wisdom to confront us again and again. The content of the sayings often reminds us of our own responsibility: we frequently meet apparently conflicting advice, and our wisdom comes in wrestling with our own situation while continuing to meditate on the sayings.

The proverb, or wise saying, is perhaps the most universal form of wisdom. It is an exquisite delight to find a new one that rings true, and most of us have our own favourites. But wisdom is passed on in many other forms too – stories, discussions, prayers, sermons, pictures, poems, catechisms, and so on. Lists have been especially popular. They are helpful ways of summing up the essentials, of examining ourselves, and of quickly reminding ourselves of basic wisdom in a new situation. They also offer a way of meditating on a balanced range of elements, perhaps in some regular cycle. Many people find that such lists are extremely valuable, and that using them has long-term effects on their moral awareness.

In the sphere of goodness, in the Western Christian tradition there have been two classic lists. The seven virtues are:

Faith
Hope
Love
Prudence
Justice
Courage
Self-control

The seven deadly sins are:

Pride
Anger
Envy/Jealousy
Greed/Avarice/Covetousness
Sloth
Lust
Gluttony

They give endless scope for meditation and self-examination. But my favourite is the 'fruit of the Spirit' list in Paul's Letter to the Galatians 5:22–23:

Love
Joy
Peace
Patience
Kindness
Goodness/Generosity
Faithfulness/Faith
Gentleness/Humility
Self-control/Temperance

That is a whole moral ecology in summary form, with the atmosphere formed by the basic act of Christian behaviour, the prayer 'Come, Holy Spirit!' Each fruit has its wisdom, and it is also fascinating to think about them in combination. What about gentle, generous self-control? Joyful patience? Peaceful, patient joy? What are the teachings and practices that can cultivate such habits? What might this list mean for relations between men and women, or for our use of money? How can each be understood through the life, death and resurrection of Jesus Christ? If all the fruits are not only in short supply but also often go against the grain of our culture, how might they be publicly demonstrated? What might a prophetic gentleness or patience be like? And if 'fruit' is a good image, how might we not only cultivate them but savour and celebrate them?

We do not get far in such questioning before we realize why the wisdom tradition has been marked by intensive discussions and debates. Distillations of wisdom invite commentary and diverse applications, and lead us into having to risk making judgements and new connections. In the Bible the wisdom tradition is not just in Proverbs, Job and Ecclesiastes, but also runs through the historical books, the prophets, the Psalms and the books of the law, and in the New Testament it is constantly appearing in the gospels and letters. This pervasiveness underlines a fundamental biblical point, in which it is joined by most other religious and philosophical traditions: it is of the utmost importance to be educated in wisdom. Any community desiring good character formation in its members will fail if it does not pay thorough attention to how people learn wisdom.

EDUCATING FOR WISDOM

So how is wisdom learnt? That is itself a matter of wisdom, and therefore is not to be laid out in formulas or programmes which can simply be put into practice. At every point, constant discernment is required about timing, selection, and all the particularities of people and situations. Yet there are certain distillations of what has been learnt in the past which we ignore at our peril.

One lesson is that wisdom is best learnt face to face by apprenticeship to those who have themselves learnt it the same way.

Perhaps the ultimate privilege is to have wise parents, teachers and friends – a wise community of the heart. Because wisdom is so much a matter of making the deep connections in the midst of the complexities of life, there is no substitute for seeing how someone does it. But, more than just seeing, it is a matter of being seen. The wise see us in our potential. They listen with the 'inner ear'. They open us up, inspire us, energize us, allow us to blossom, and give us a sense that there is always more. Excellence is the aim, yet they are patient with us. It is a gentle, utterly respectful overwhelming, at the heart of which is delight in truth and goodness. The classic sign of this is immense gratitude, increasing as the wisdom is tested and developed, together with the desire to pass it on.

So another lesson is that the channels through which wisdom is passed on are of crucial importance to everyone. If they are clogged, polluted or shallow then the whole moral ecology is affected. I think of all those rich streams that flow through history – Socrates to Plato to Aristotle and beyond, the great schools of Hinduism and Buddhism, the ulamas and Sufis of Islam, the centuries of Jewish rabbinic discussion, the theologies and spiritualities of Christianity in its many forms, the many largely ignored traditions of wisdom in oppressed peoples and cultures, and the depths embodied in the arts and literature. These are our 'life-giving lines', and Micheal O'Siadhail describes one of them in 'Homage':

Nearly eighty, slow-paced,
stooped, he enters. Even his suit
has seen better days; but touching
that instrument, his face is chamois

which puckers, ripples each phrase;
a smile inscrutable, ears pricked
for an inward zing, heard deep
in the calm of age. This virtuoso

Vlado Perlmuter a half-century
ago, Ravel's apprentice, played
these pieces for the maître whom
in his turn Fauré had fostered.

Lineage of love, strange dynasty
beyond the blood, every succession
wills on the gift; a current
skips from fingertip to tip

along life-giving lines, as once,
suddenly, thumbing through a treasury
we find ourselves, stumble on
forerunners who forefather us.

Warmed by homage, a melody resung
reddens again the afterglow;
son to many far-flung fathers,
there are sons who watch for you.[2]

It is hard to see any educational process that should take priority over wisdom's 'lineage of love, strange dynasty/ beyond the blood'. O'Siadhail sees it as a form of parenting, and in the penultimate line faces his own responsibility in gratitude to his 'many far-flung fathers'.

But what are in fact the priorities of our educational institutions? They pursue many worthy aims – information, knowledge, meaning, skills, personal development, and more. But it might be that more intensive attention to those aims actually makes the system less hospitable to a wisdom which has to do with the shaping of lives, families, and the various other spheres of society. Within whose speciality do those complex, interrelated issues fall? The currently fashionable thing is to identify them as issues of 'values' or 'ethics'. This is a step in the right direction, but usually fails because values are cut off from their environment in ecologies of beliefs, practices and specific traditions of wisdom. Above all there is resistance to any hint that here we enter a realm of multiple overwhelming in which we have to swim in wisdom. If we try to stay in control through information, knowledge and skills, keeping our feet safely on the bottom of the ocean, we drown. So we see an educational system drowning in information, knowledge and skills, and rarely even attending to the question: how can we learn and teach wisdom?

A third lesson is, therefore, to create and sustain settings for education in which wisdom can flourish in face-to-face apprenticeship, without detracting from other worthy educational aims. The basic setting remains the family, but all other institutions and communities face the same challenge. It is one of the supreme delights to find, from time to time, a business that seems wisely managed; a church where fresh wisdom for our times is being minted; or a school where, against many pressures, encouragement and opportunity is given to pupils to swim freely in one of the great wisdom traditions.

A final lesson is about the education given by life. Gordon Jackson writes about

> Wisdom that is the art of making
> good out of what life throws at us.[3]

At New Year 1943, a few months before he was arrested, and two years before his execution for taking part in the plot against Hitler, Dietrich Bonhoeffer wrote a fifteen-page 'Reckoning' called 'After Ten Years', looking back on the lessons learnt by him and his friends and comrades during the period of Nazi rule in Germany. It is a classic gem of wisdom compacted under intense pressure as he and others resisted the Nazis in Church and State. It is a story of ordinary ethics and virtues being overwhelmed and having to risk new forms of action without precedent.

He asks 'Who stands fast?' in such an extreme situation. His answer is: the responsible person, who tries to make his or her whole life 'an answer to the question and call of God'.[4] He contrasts obedience to abstract principles with taking 'our share of responsibility for the moulding of history in every situation and at every moment, whether we are the victors or the vanquished'.[5] Central to his concern is the ethical importance of wisdom. Foolishness is 'a more dangerous enemy to the good than evil'. The only real cure for it is 'a person's inward liberation to live a responsible life before God'.[6] He offers his wisdom on justice, God's action in history, trust, the sense of quality, sympathy, large-heartedness, the way to approach the future, insecurity and death. But he recognizes that 'most people learn wisdom only from personal experience', and perhaps his most moving statement comes at the very end, under the heading 'The view from below':

> There remains an experience of incomparable value. We have for once learnt to see the great events of world history from below, from the perspective of the outcast, the suspects, the maltreated, the powerless, the oppressed, the reviled – in short, from the perspective of those who suffer. The important thing is that

neither bitterness nor envy should have gnawed at the heart during this time, that we should have come to look with new eyes at matters great and small, sorrow and joy, strength and weakness, that our perception of generosity, humanity, justice and mercy should have become clearer, freer, less corruptible. We have to learn that personal suffering is a more effective key, a more rewarding principle for exploring the world in thought and action than personal good fortune. This perspective from below must not become the partisan possession of those who are eternally dissatisfied; rather, we must do justice to life in all its dimensions from a higher satisfaction, whose foundation is beyond any talk of 'from below' or 'from above'. This is the way in which we may affirm it.[7]

That balanced statement, made long before the 'option for the poor' in Latin American liberation theology and the priority of the standpoint of the oppressed advocated by a range of other theologies, remains as a fundamental insight into the formative role of suffering. We will look at this more fully in chapter 6 later. But there is a wisdom of joy as well as of suffering, which chapter 7 will explore, including Bonhoeffer's contribution to it.

I conclude with two wisdom stories by Donald Nicholl.

A STORY OF IRRESPONSIBILITY

Nicholl tells the following story, set in Edinburgh during the 1950s:

I was visiting my friend, Dr Guth Badenoch, one afternoon at his home in George Square, and I mentioned to him how sad

I was over the death of a child in the operating theatre of the nearby hospital. I then went on to say that I felt great sympathy for the doctor who had been in charge of the operation since he had encountered an unexpected complication and could hardly be blamed for what had eventually happened. To my astonishment Dr Badenoch, a just and understanding man, replied, 'Oh, I don't know about that, Donald. I think the man is to blame. If anybody had handed me ether instead of chloroform I would have known from the weight that it was the wrong thing. You see, I know the man well. We were students together at Aberdeen, and he could have become one of the finest surgeons in Europe if only he had given his mind to it. But he didn't. He was more interested in golf. So he just used to do enough work to pass his examinations and no more. And that's how he has lived his life – just enough to get through, but no more; so he has never picked up those seemingly peripheral bits of knowledge that can one day be crucial. The other day in that theatre a bit of "peripheral" knowledge was crucial and he didn't have it. But it wasn't the other day that he failed – it was thirty years ago, when he only gave himself half-heartedly to medicine.' It goes without saying that I found Dr Badenoch's words a hard comment, and I do not know whether in this particular case they were justified. But fundamentally he was right: for almost a lifetime we may project an image of ourselves that enables us to get through, that deceives others and may even deceive ourselves. In the end, however, what we **are** always comes out; it is for what we are that we are responsible.[8]

A STORY OF RESPONSIBILITY AND JOY

At the end of his profound little book *Holiness,* Donald Nicholl reflects on what the New Testament Letter of James says about the destructive capacity of the tongue, and he tells of the impact on himself of a classic Jewish treatise on evil speech (*loshon hora*), *Guard Your Tongue* by Reb Yisroel Meir:

> But of all the unrelenting demands made by the discipline of the tongue none stood me in such good stead as the one which forbids you to refer in any way to some wrong which another may have done towards you even though it was wrong beyond a doubt.
>
> What made this example so applicable to my own situation was my having discovered by accident certain hurtful remarks (*loshon hora*) which had been made about myself by one or two scholars at a period when they were malcontent. During the following months numerous occasions presented themselves to me, especially in intellectual discussions, when at least on the surface I might quite legitimately have revealed the incompetence of each of them. However, every time I was tempted to do so there would arise before my eyes the stern portrait of Reb Yisroel displayed on the cover of *Guard Your Tongue.* Immediately I would be seized by the fear of God; and so I refrained from saying anything. Silence, I realized, is also an alternative, for 'nothing in the whole universe is so like unto God as silence'. Very soon even the voice of temptation went silent.
>
> The reward came several months later, almost at the end of the academic year. At dinner one night I felt a wonderfully deep sense of peace and affection and joy flowing from one to another of those of us sharing the same table. Then suddenly

I remembered that my table companions constituted the very group that had spoken harshly of me some months earlier. Yet now they were full of affection and warmth. With a shudder I realized that this wonderful fellowship would have been quite impossible if I had said one such word as I was tempted to say. I made a silent prayer of thanks to God and called a blessing upon Reb Yisroel.[9]

FOUR

SECRETS AND DISCIPLINES – SOUL-SHAPING

Life is riddled with secrecy. There are secrets in every area – family, politics, business, medicine, and all relationships that are about anything important. In the course of a single day we might use an E-mail password on our computer and our PIN number on a cash machine, have a telephone conversation with a colleague which is definitely not for broadcasting, listen to a friend's agonies over an intimate relationship, visit a doctor about pains which no one else knows about, work on a confidential project, take part in planning a surprise birthday party for someone, and write in our journal what we really felt during the day. Vast areas of what goes on in society are concealed behind labels of security, confidentiality or privacy. The media thrive on revealing secrets. An immense amount of energy, ingenuity and money is devoted to keeping secrets, and also to uncovering them.

Secrecy tends to have a bad name. That is mainly because it is such a powerful and pervasive feature of life and is therefore, like money or sex or communication skills, a prime target for corruption and manipulation. Anyone who does something bad or criminal will of course want to conceal the fact, and secrecy is essential to deception, hypocrisy and other ways of misleading people.

Yet secrecy is also essential to our best relationships. It plays a major role in living within the multiple good and bad overwhelmings of life, and it is vital for the health of any society or group. What we have done, or what we know or think or suspect or feel or hope or fear, is not by any means necessarily to be communicated to everyone or perhaps to anyone; or maybe it is to be shared not now but later. We are always having to think before we speak and make complicated judgements about confidentiality and the effects of disclosure. This, at its simplest, gives the theme of this chapter: it is about secrets and the disciplines they require. Dealing with secrets shapes the most intimate aspect of our self which we call our soul. And as modern psychology and psychoanalysis have stressed, many of our life-shaping secrets are ones we are not even conscious of – they are repressed, forgotten, denied and deposited in our unconscious. Our disciplines of living must take account of these depths too.

SECRETS OF INTIMACY

In intimate relationships it is constantly surprising that the deeper we become involved the more mysterious the other can seem. Micheal O'Siadhail in 'Revelation' describes a moment after twenty-one years of living with one 'stranger and lover':

Our train gains ground in the evening light.
Among the trees the sun catches in its fall
Glints and anglings of a stone in a distant gable,
A broadcast of facets, one and infinite.
I glance at you. There's so much unexplained.
Plays of your light keep provoking my infinity;
Already something in your presence overflows me,
A gleam of a face refusing to be contained.

How little I know of you. Again and again
I've resolved to be the giver and not the taker,
Somehow to surpass myself. Am I the mapmaker
So soon astray in this unknowable terrain?
Twenty-one years. And I'm journeying to discover
Only what your face reveals. Stranger and lover.[1]

At the heart of a relationship like this is something neither partner
can ever encompass. It cannot be contained or explained, and is
expressed in the simultaneous openness yet elusiveness of face,
eyes, speech and touch. This is the secret between two people, and
it can go on getting deeper for decades. Maturing love finds that
its secrets and its disciplines multiply.

Why is this? We are secrets to ourselves, let alone to another.
Every day and night together leaves so much unexpressed and
unexplained. How can the significance of just one smile, or one
bitter row, be articulated? We constantly come up against the
sheer otherness and difference of each other. And we do not just
have to do with an individual, but with the community in his or
her heart, and all the secrets of those relationships. Deep love
inspires deep love beyond its own face to face – for friends, children, 'the faceless'. Each time this happens the trust of the original
lovers is tested. Their own love is transformed by the new loves.
They have to trust that the new secrets between them, made up of
all the unspoken and inexpressible things that are going on in
other relationships, are good secrets and do not compete with or
devalue their own.

What are good secrets? They are those which are kept for the
good of other people or because the time is not right for them to
be told or because they are simply inexpressible. Some seeds need
a long germination time, and great sensitivity is needed in probing

or unearthing them. Without trust that the secrets of the other are good, the relationship either ceases to deepen and becomes fossilized, or it is destroyed by jealousy. Jealousy has a rooted suspicion of the secrets of the other. Secrets intensify both trust and betrayal: to respect a partner's reserve about their intimate life can multiply trust; but it also allows scope for terrible deceit. Jealousy and possessiveness cannot sustain this trust and try to violate the secrets of the other.

In 'Secrets of Assisi', an extraordinary recreation of the intimacy between St Francis and St Clare (and also drawing on that between Abelard and Heloïse), set in the Secret Garden in Assisi, Micheal O'Siadhail has Francis say to Clare:

The closer we are, the more secrets we need.

The final stanza is a rich, subtle weave of the wisdom of mature love and its necessary secrets:

Beyond the lavender, the buddleia and the roses,
Behind a darker screen of trees that closes
Over bequeathed secrets we learn to repossess
In hints and traces, those words we must guess
Or thoughts which ricochet, the echoes and signs,
Riddles of what we read between the lines,
This tick-tack of things we still negotiate,
The silent interplay where we'll translate
Those unheard words that in a heart betoken
All of all which must remain unspoken.
High in the upper partials of our loyal past,
Those Umbrian voices ring true and steadfast
Across our common heritage of predicaments

As we travel in turn beyond a first innocence
To comb and choose what each needs to reveal,
To count veils and know the heart may conceal
As much as it discloses and yet not harden
Or grow suave. In green shadows of this garden
When lovers withdraw, in moments out of sight
And mind, beyond the busy open sunlight
Out in louder days where lives go on,
I broker faithful secrets between the gone.[2]

Francis and Clare are a classic case of intimacy and 'faithful secrets' sustained by a rigorous discipline – in their case prayer, celibacy, obedience to a radically demanding vocation and, through all that, celebration of their friendship in the Spirit. They are like a laboratory of the soul in which we can glimpse in specially pure conditions what happens when wholehearted intimacy, reserve and discipline are combined in mutual trust.

If intimacy generates secrets even between those directly involved, then how much more is it largely secret from third parties. This need not come from any desire to be exclusive or from deliberate concealment. It is more intrinsic than that. It is simply that the ongoing occurrence of intimacy would have to be participated in to be understood, and that is by definition impossible. What happens in intimacy, whether in twos, threes or more, cannot be communicated adequately to those not part of it. It therefore has the character of a secret, something known to be there but also known to have a great deal that remains unknown. The only adequate revelation of it would be to take part in a repeat performance – but of course any repetition would not be the original thing and would be changed by the new participant. And if, in some miraculous way, we were to have access to the secrets of the intimacy of others we would come up against the even more fundamental secrets between the participants that, as we have seen, are part of any mature loving. So between intimates there exist, in O'Siadhail's words, 'riddles of what we read between the lines', 'all which must remain unspoken', 'veils' over the heart; but to outsiders all this is intensified and multiplied.

Yet there is also something about the secrets of intimacy that makes us want to share them. We thirst for deeper penetration into the depths of others, and to have someone with whom we can share our own secrets and who can understand us more deeply. Every branch of the media shows how widespread and insatiable this desire is: 'kiss and tell' stories, invasions of privacy, an endless stream of novels, films and television programmes on sex, love, family life. All of that can get the desire to share secrets a bad name, but again it is a case of 'the corruption of the best is the worst'. At root the desire to be able to share in the secrets of intimacy is good. We rightly sense that at its best there is something here so rich that, treated sensitively, revealing it uncovers new layers and new dimensions.

It is not just one static secret. The secrecy is dynamic. It is better called a mystery. The attempt to communicate it leads to astonishment at its inexhaustibility and reveals its capacity to invite into new depths. Who ever fathoms the eyes of a lover? As O'Siadhail says elsewhere:

Me – know you? So utterly more
different than the same. A modesty
absent in its presence, glory of desire;
something revealed, then drawn away.'

A mystery like this is secret and inaccessible because of its sheer abundance and the overwhelming, inexpressible dynamic of love. It is too big to be known. It eludes us by being beyond us – O'Siadhail in 'Revelation' speaks of 'infinity': 'something in your presence overflows me'. When faced with this dynamic secrecy of mystery, how do we cope? I have already discussed some of the virtues that are called for and the vices that are always tempting. But a further dimension of coping is to learn the disciplines of intimacy.

DISCIPLINES OF INTIMACY

As lovers we long to express love. We search for adequate words, send letters, buy presents, and show our love in dozens of non-verbal ways. We reach out to intensive and expansive forms of communication such as touch, music, dance, and poetry. Through those love can be imagined, explored and enjoyed. In other words, one of the basic disciplines of intimacy is that of communication.

Communication in intimacy takes on a great urgency and even risk. When and how should I say what I feel? What questions should I ask? What are the limits, in physical or emotional intimacy, or in commitment? What should be shared with others? But surrounding and underlying all those is the central mystery of the other person and of what is happening between us. Here the communication problem cannot be removed. It stretches all our capacities, and we draw on the best that others have produced in order to try to do it justice. Yet without constantly attempting to do some sort of justice to the mystery we are disloyal to it, and fail to be fully alive to the other person.

What sort of discipline is this? (I use 'discipline' to mean a practice or habit which it is helpful to develop in order to shape our lives better.) It is a discipline which first of all recognizes that it cannot cope: it cannot master the reality it is engaged with. It acknowledges that it is overwhelmed and will always remain so: the mystery of another person is not a problem to be solved so as to pass on to the next problem. So within this mystery we stretch our minds, bodies, hearts and imaginations in order to express to ourselves, to the beloved, to other people and to God what this reality is. It is clearly a discipline of the whole person. It needs to be sensitive to what O'Siadhail calls the 'hints and traces', 'the echoes and signs' in which the mystery is veiled. It will be a discipline of language, imagination and behaviour (all behaviour is communication) that respects the reserve of others, their boundaries and their differences.

There are terrible distortions and violations of intimacy in pornography, media purchases of 'tell all' stories, and much 'graphic' fiction in novels or films. But there are also good testimonies to intimacy. They can be found in all the arts and in all media. An intimacy which is disciplined, in the sense of being vigilant about the right and wrong crossing of boundaries, seeks out those good testimonies, feeds on them and then generates its own. It is such high-quality communication that sustains and enhances the dignity and open mystery of love.

I have been using Micheal O'Siadhail's poetry as one example of such testimony. It is the outcome of years of dedication to his art. Its response to being overwhelmed is to generate fresh poetry in new combinations of words and forms. Each poem is itself a disciplined structure in which metre, rhyme, assonance, images, thoughts, and overall form (the sonnet form in 'Revelation', for example) converge to try to do justice to the theme. Each detail matters; and so, through the overwhelming and the details, the shape of the poem emerges. The discipline of poetry-writing is a highly developed, millennia-old way of helping to shape life. It calls the rest of us non-poets to two disciplines in response: to the discipline of high-quality attention to what poets write, including learning some poems by heart; and to comparable dedication to high-quality communication in our own ways.

What are our own ways? Singing (the most popular form in which poetry is spread), music-making, lovemaking, smiles, gestures, ways of touching, humour, doing things together, making things, cooking, sport, a good cause, hospitality of many sorts – all these and innumerable other activities can be joyful disciplines in the service of intimacy or inspired by it. In them we see the extraordinary dynamic of 'faithful secrets'. They invite us deeper into the joyful and sorrowful mysteries of intimacy – think of singing together, or sexual intercourse, or shared meals. At the same time they draw us into fresh communication, and become the hidden inspiration of countless things we do, say and suffer. They are soul-shaping.

In another poem about St Francis and St Clare, O'Siadhail savours the puzzle of their relationship, and also introduces the discipline of communication that is at the heart of Christian intimacy – prayer:

My Clare, in years to come they'll
puzzle over us! *Francesco e Chiara.*
I can almost hear them chuckle.
Let them wonder! If they don't know
that love's first sight can seal
a lifetime, how will they understand?
You came to me when I already

was sworn to Mistress Poverty.
Saints carry their souls in lovely
vessels, only iron wills have made
our rule. There's a thousand ways
to know another; we may not share
the daily buzz and flittings of a mind.
Each alone in prayer acclaims this love,
still in the cell of its first perfection.[4]

BEING INTIMATE WITH GOD –
SECRETS AND DISCIPLINES

Much of the previous sections on intimacy between people has close parallels to our intimacy with God, and the last poem about Francis and Clare unites the two. On the one hand, God is radically intimate, 'closer to us than we are to ourselves', a mystery that we never fathom. On the other hand, God inspires overflowing communication in praise, thanks, complaints, and prayer of all sorts, as well as endless other activities. God is the life of the soul, and is the secret of the world and of each person. Both types of intimacy and overflow, relating to other people and to God, come together beautifully in Thomas Mann's portrayal of Jacob in his biblical novel, *Joseph and his Brothers*. Jacob at the end of his life talks about his wife Rachel: 'Anyhow, he simply loved to speak of her, even when there was no point at all – just as he loved to speak of God.'[5]

Jesus tied the two intimacies together in his love for God and in calling his followers to be his friends. In previous chapters we have explored how he shaped his life in the face of the overwhelming reality of God, but now we need to notice a further dimension: his insistence on the secret discipline of prayer.

In the Sermon on the Mount Jesus taught:

> And when you pray, you must not be like the hypocrites; for they love to stand and pray in the synagogues and at the street corners, that they may be seen of people. Truly, I say to you, they have received their reward. But when you pray, go into your room and shut the door and pray to your Father who is in secret; and your Father who sees in secret will reward you. (Matthew 6:5–6)

This is obviously a basic discipline of intimacy with God. Dietrich Bonhoeffer wrote about these verses:

> Prayer is the supreme instance of the hidden character of the Christian life. It is the antithesis of self-display. When people pray, they have ceased to know themselves, and know only God whom they call upon. Prayer does not aim at any direct effect on the world; it is addressed to God alone, and is therefore the perfect example of undemonstrative action.[6]

Jesus took part in synagogue and Temple worship – he was an observant Jew who seems to have followed the usual prayer and worship disciplines of his religion. But there is also something beyond those which was of the greatest importance in the distinctive shape of his life. It is as if, corresponding to his recognition of the reality of the overwhelming abundance and generosity of God and of his own overwhelming responsibility for the Kingdom of God, he had to have secret disciplines through which he engaged with God. This sort of God and this Kingdom of God simply could not be coped with by routine methods. So the gospels have many indications of Jesus's own secret life with God: forty days alone in the wilderness, nights spent in prayer, the prayer on the mountain of his transfiguration, and the agony in the Garden of Gethsemane.

There is a vital lesson here, which is always in need of being relearnt. At its heart is the simple truth that a God of overwhelming is best engaged with through practices that allow us to be overwhelmed. What does that mean?

One thing it does *not* mean is throwing overboard routines or patterns of prayer, meditation or study. I remember the transformation in my prayer when an old Anglican monk explained the wisdom of following a particular pattern of prayer and Bible readings – a 'daily office'. I have not always kept to it, and the form has changed over the years, but ever since then it has been like a basic rhythm of life in good and bad times. Being (more or less) faithful to it has formed life in all sorts of often barely perceptible ways, and has sometimes been the opening for significant developments. But, even more importantly, such habits help to shape the unconscious, those layers of self where the sediment of the past is deposited and which nourish (or pollute) our instincts, intuitions and reactions.

The wisdom of following a regular prayer pattern is basic to most traditions. There is a realism about it which knows that to let our prayer depend on 'feeling like doing it' is foolish. It is a long-term formative thing, and we need to take it on trust from others that it will be worthwhile giving it a try for a few years. If we persevere that long, it will probably become a 'good compulsion'.

Good routines are the framework for appropriate overwhelmings. The classic example of this is the Church Year. Most days are ordinary, but there are also the feasts and fasts. These are the public, community forms of being overwhelmed. They show the basic wisdom of not trying to keep life always balanced and on an even keel: we need the extremes and the excesses, the carnivals. There is an intensity about wholehearted feasting and fasting which transforms us in ways that steady routine cannot.

But even the feasts and fasts can become routine, and history is full of new inspirations for ways of allowing God to overwhelm us. Here are seven which seem to be specially appropriate in our society, though they all have deep pre-modern roots. They are practices of excess which go beyond the routine and try to plunge into and explore the infinite secret riches of God.

PRACTICES OF EXCESS

Praying as long as it takes

In a culture of busyness it is easy for believers just to give God some slots in the diary and after them to go on to the next thing. That is of course how we mostly have to live. But from time to time (probably best not regularly) when we go into our room, shut the door and pray in secret, it is a good idea to allow God as long as God wants. How long is that? Who knows? But it would be surprising if a God of such abundance, who longs to communicate in love, could be satisfied with brief set times. It is easy to find ourselves treating God less generously than we treat our best friend, our spouse or even our customers. In all those relationships we recognize occasions when whatever is going on has to take as long as it takes. This is part of the unpredictability of life: we are not in control, and if we try to set limits in advance and cut off too soon we may miss out on something vital.

So every now and then it is worth having open-ended prayer in secret. This could mean clearing a day and starting to pray in the morning. More likely it means starting in the evening and being willing to go on all night. People do it occasionally for parties or for televised live sports events, and parents are frequently up for as long as it takes to get a baby to sleep. So why not with God too? Jesus's nights in prayer do not seem to have been regular, but given his intimacy with God there is something natural about them.

Open-ended prayer allows for innovations that do not fit elsewhere in our lives. We might savour one name of God after another. We might linger over past years of our life in order to thank God or repent. The Bible or a liturgy or some other text can be read slowly, with time to meditate whenever we like. We might 'pray with our pen', writing in a journal. A complex situation can be considered at leisure before God. Various postures and gestures can be used. We can let Sister Wendy Beckett guide us in appreciating some paintings. One person after another can be prayed for – a whole extended family, or a workforce, or a school. There can be conversation with Jesus, or silence, or shouting, or singing. It does not matter if attention wanders or even if we drop off to sleep – there is time to wake up and to pick up the thread again.

It is likely that there will be at least as many ways of filling such times as there are ways of being intimate with those we love. And one of the repeated discoveries of such vigils is that there is no competition between intimacy with God and with other people. On the contrary, it is in such times that we relate most deeply to other people, and frequently find our relationships transformed in the process. We tend to develop a taste for these extended prayer times, and expand them into periods completely away from routine so that prayer can take even longer. Retreats are the commonest way of doing this. It is no accident that in a society of intensifying multiple overwhelmings the retreat movement is flourishing.

Intensive time away with other people

At the key turning-point in his ministry, after which he oriented himself towards Jerusalem and death, Jesus took his disciples into strange territory and then climbed with the three closest up a high mountain to pray. There they had the extraordinary experience of the transfiguration, an intense mystery in which prayer, the transfigured face and clothes of Jesus, an engulfing cloud, the voice of God, and conversation with key figures of the Old Testament came together.

Small groups that seek God and God's desires together have been at the heart of most of the major developments in the Church over the centuries. They have also been fundamental to its ordinary flourishing, and they continue to be the most important single level of church life – from families, Methodist classes, mission teams and prayer meetings to youth groups, committees and 'base communities'. Whenever such a group breaks out of routine and has an intensive time together or with others, then transformations tend to happen.

Similar things happen in different ways in larger groups. Jesus was a specialist in these, and provoked crowds to extend their time listening to him. They were clearly gripped by someone for whom they would stay away from home for longer than planned, with no provision for food. Large numbers of people first become Christians or are sustained and renewed through holiday camps, house parties, conferences and festivals. It is also fascinating to see the rapid growth of pilgrimages, which have been a classic way to get involved in an improvised community dedicated to God. Inner change happens more readily in settings like that. But try to explain afterwards what happened, and the mystery of it is apparent.

Giving generously and secretly

Jesus was outrageous in his attitude to possessions. He was quite clear that we should give with a double discipline: generously and secretly. We are to give with the generosity of God, and we are not to let our left hand know what our right hand is doing. This secret 'discipline of excess' is perhaps the most transformative of all. The 'conversion of the pocket' has always been seen as a critical test of the conversion of heart and mind. The secret of Jesus's secret generosity is clear: radical trust in a God who knows what we need (Matthew 6:32). No more need be said – more needs to be given!

Music

There is a remarkable passage in the Letter to the Ephesians about combatting and overwhelming one form of excess with another.

> Do not get drunk with wine, for that is debauchery; but be filled with the Spirit, addressing one another in psalms and hymns and spiritual songs, singing and making melody to the Lord with all your heart [or, in your heart], always and for everything giving thanks in the name of our Lord Jesus Christ to God the Father. (Ephesians 5:18–20)

Music is a powerful way of being overwhelmed. It surrounds us, engulfs us, goes right through us. It can raise spirits, change moods, create atmospheres. Music binds groups together. It can overwhelm with loudness but also with lullabies. Ephesians encourages the 'sober drunkenness' of singing selves. What if we were really to follow its instruction? Wouldn't the whole atmosphere of our lives change? The letter goes on immediately to talk of marriages and household life: we are invited to be singing husbands and wives, parents and children. All of the great Christian desires, truths and images are embodied in music and song. Singing is ideally suited to the fact that they are so overwhelming. It keeps them vibrant and yet mysterious, the music always pointing beyond the words to further dimensions. It is hard to put our finger on the difference between saying something and singing it, but we feel that a good tune adds something to the sense and also lets the words sound more richly in our hearts and minds.

It is worth reflecting on the three types of singing to the Lord that Ephesians mentions. Psalms are the great classic songs to God, sung century after century all round the world, the common hymn book of Jews and Christians. Many of them are about being overwhelmed with joy, praise, thanks, suffering, fear or remorse. Hymns are probably the sort of song we have in our actual hymn books, a range from different periods, with each community having its favourites. But what are 'spiritual songs'? They are most likely what is sometimes called 'singing in the Spirit', when an individual or group improvises 'in tongues'. I have been in congregations where this happens, and it is an unforgettable form of inspired overwhelming, as voices blend and harmonize without a score or a conductor.

The Jesus Prayer

> Lord Jesus Christ, Son of God,
> Have mercy on me.

That little 'Jesus Prayer' (and variations on it) has an extraordinary history. It has been repeated countless times by countless people, has shaped the lives of whole communities, and now is practised around the world in a wide variety of churches, by individuals and by groups.

The prayer is exquisitely simple yet extraordinarily embracing. Simon Barrington-Ward, an Anglican bishop, writes:

> It is as I have been through the exercise of the Jesus Prayer – and really only through this – that I have gradually seen more and more how totally this recognition of what we are, *and* of what we have in us to be, is held together within the recollection of God's loving presence in the words 'Lord Jesus Christ, Son of God...' and then the longing cry of the prayer: 'Have mercy on me...'
>
> That cry is so much more than just grovelling over my sins. It is a longing for a transformation, both an inner and an outer transformation, a transformation within the microcosm of my own heart and the macrocosm of the universe...
>
> As I have prayed the Jesus Prayer continuously, morning and evening, it has begun to start 'praying itself', as it were; at other times, both in the night and in the day, at odd moments, walking or cycling, in the car, or even in the stillness between two conversations, it has assumed more and more the form of some kind of a universal rhythm. The stream of the loving purpose encapsulated in the prayer seems gradually to be uniting the prayer with all the tragic struggles of our world and of wounded nature itself. It seems to make the person who is praying a part of that movement of new creation.[7]

This is the opposite of the 'vain repetitions' the Sermon on the Mount warns against (Matthew 6:7). The Jesus Prayer is like a lover repeatedly naming the beloved, or the person over-whelmed with gratitude saying 'Thank you, thank you, thank you...' It is a way of paying attention to an infinite mystery, slowly growing into it so that it is inhabited consciously and unconsciously.

Bible study

My favourite verse in the Bible is 2 Corinthians 4:6. I once mentioned this to a colleague, Professor Frances Young, and said that some day, perhaps in retirement, I would love to write a book on 2 Corinthians. She went home, re-read the letter, and next morning I found a note in my pigeonhole: 'When do we begin our book on 2 Corinthians?' This began many years of joint study of the letter, holding seminars on it, translating it, reading some of the vast literature about it and writing the book *Meaning and Truth in 2 Corinthians*. It was an extraordinary experience to be able to take so much time, without even a deadline, on one quite short letter. At the end of it the letter seemed deeper, richer in meaning and far more powerful than when we began. We had proposed answers to some of the 'problems' of the letter, but the letter itself was not a problem to be solved or explained. My favourite verse too had gained in depth and breadth, but I felt as if we had only scratched its surface – even after focusing much of the last two chapters of the book on it!

Study like this is extravagant in time and energy. It meets the excess of meaning in the text with a practice of excess, exploring it in one way after another, alone and in groups, and then acknowl-edging the surplus still remaining. I have found the same aston-ishing, surging life of the Bible in a home group in inner-city

Birmingham: week after week it opened us up to God, ourselves and our situations.

Silence

Silence can be seen as the perfection of secrecy and of discipline together. There are at least as many types of silence as there are of speech. Silence as a practice of excess is above all a recognition that language and even music are overwhelmed by mystery.

Scattered through speech and music are pauses, gaps between words and notes that allow them to make sense and patterns rather than merge together in chaos. Mystery rightly generates more and more speech and music. That is one way in which the endlessness of mystery can be explored. But intensity of involvement in mystery also inspires silence in fuller and more disciplined ways. Pauses and gaps can become still points of convergence and overflow. The quality of our silence transforms our listening, speaking and singing. But silence also allows for a surplus that is not articulated. There is an overwhelming abundance in which we are immersed and which calls for practices of silence.

In the face of the good and bad overwhelmings (what the Christian theological tradition has sometimes called the dark and bright mysteries, each unfathomable in different ways) we all know how inadequate our words are. Faced with acute suffering, horrific evil or immense joy, we sense that any words have to come from an encompassing silence. But that does not just happen as a matter of course. Many things in ourselves and our culture resist or even destroy our capacity for such silence. We therefore need the wisdom on silence that religious traditions have learnt by long experience.

It begins with a discipline of the tongue in the interests of doing justice to mystery. Baron von Hügel wrote to his niece:

> Be silent about great things, let them grow inside you. Never discuss them: discussion is so limiting and distracting. It makes things grow smaller. You think you swallow things when they ought to swallow you. Before all greatness, be silent – in art, in music, in religion: silence.[8]

Beyond that principle of allowing greatness to 'swallow' us, we need to do it. Sit still for long enough. Allow ourselves to have time in the presence of a text, an icon, a thought, a situation, a person, God. We soon find that full silence is something that affects our whole self. We become more aware of our body with its restlessness, of our mind with its distractions, of our heart with its passions and fantasies. Silence is a niche in the 'ecology of self' which is affected by all the other niches. But it also affects all the others, and slowly the atmosphere of our whole ecology changes as we practise it (even sporadically!).

Nor is silence just an individual matter. Groups and whole communities can learn the fruitfulness of silence. It is an immensely important but largely hidden tradition in the Church, usually practised in monastic and other specially dedicated communities. Only the Quakers have made silence a key element in public worship. But many others taste it and long for more. In that inner-city Birmingham home group one of the most remarkable experiences was of growing in the ability to wait in silence together before God. The silence was in itself an honouring of who God is. It was also the secret of a vivid reception of the Bible and a fresh minting of praise, prayer and practical wisdom to be shared.

THE SECRET DISCIPLINE OF LOVE: ST THÉRÈSE'S SMILE

There is one practice of excess on which all the rest depend: love. Jesus on the cross represents the extreme of extravagant loving. But what might that mean in ordinary life? Thérèse of Lisieux died in 1897 aged twenty-four, having been a nun in a convent dedicated to prayer since she was fifteen. Within a few years millions of people were asking that she be acknowledged a saint by the Roman Catholic Church, which happened in 1925. Yet during her final illness Thérèse overheard one of her fellow nuns say: 'Sister Thérèse will die soon; what will our Mother Prioress be able to write in her obituary notice? She entered our convent, lived and died – there really is no more to say.' Why was there more?

At the heart of her life and of the teaching which emerged through the publication of her autobiography (which she had written in obedience to a request of the Prioress) was what she called her 'little way'. It involves 'only one thing': 'to strew before Jesus the flowers of little sacrifices ... expecting everything from the good God'. It is a way of the utmost simplicity, based on two truths: it is always right to love as Jesus loved; and God delights to give the capacity to love like that. The distinctive discipline that accompanied this was one of endless alertness to the requirements of love in daily life, and, at the same time, 'the veil of the smile'.

She took literally the Sermon on the Mount's instructions that you are not to let a discipline such as fasting show in your face (Matthew 6:16–18). So she concealed with her smile little and larger self-denials and sacrifices for the sake of others, and minor and sometimes major physical sufferings. Forty years after her death the surviving nuns from the convent always spoke first of her beautiful, radiant smile.

Her smile can easily be misunderstood. It could be seen as hypocritical, a pretence of happiness and of love towards the other, or as a form of politeness which conceals. But Ida Görres in her perceptive biography of Thérèse gives a sensitive analysis that is convincing: 'To Thérèse her smile was simply honest fulfilment of her vocation.'⁹

There is a famous passage in her autobiography in which she tells how her vocation came clear. She had been overwhelmed by 'infinite desires', and longed to serve Jesus by being, among other things, Carmelite, mother, warrior, priest, apostle, doctor, martyr, papal guard, prophet. Then after meditating on 1 Corinthians 13 on love as the 'more excellent way' she saw it:

> I understood that LOVE COMPRISED ALL VOCATIONS, THAT LOVE WAS EVERYTHING, THAT IT EMBRACED ALL TIMES AND PLACES ... IN A WORD, THAT IT WAS ETERNAL!
>
> Then, in the excess of my delirious joy, I cried out: O Jesus, my Love ... my vocation, at last I have found it ... MY VOCATION IS LOVE!¹⁰

Her smile embodied this vocation. It is her response to living before the face of Jesus Christ. She had a lifelong devotion to 'the Holy Face', especially the hidden, suffering face of Jesus. As she wrote in a poem: 'For Him I love I wish my smile to shine.'¹¹ She wants to smile for him and also to imitate his hiddenness. 'Beneath that smile she sacrificed things profound and valid: the basic human longing for recognition, for another's understanding look into one's own heart.'¹² Faced with other people (and Görres' account makes it clear what a very testing environment Thérèse's convent was for the practice of love), the smile recognizes that each person is made in the image of God and is to be genuinely delighted in as such – 'young Thérèse set about mastering this hidden reality of God in her fellow human beings'.[13]

Thérèse's 'veil of the smile' is a union of secrecy and discipline, single-mindedly focused on the person and love of Jesus Christ, and practised at the heart of ordinary life. It is a way 'little' enough to fit into every other way, a vocation that therefore can be at the heart of all vocations.

L'ARCHE: WAITING FOR THE BEAUTY

Communities too have their secrets and disciplines. Any community, especially one that embraces many dimensions of life such as a family, church or nation, has mysteries at its heart. Just because these mysteries are so rich, powerful and life-shaping they make great demands. They require disciplines, sometimes rigorous and highly specialized, to keep them vital and generative. What use are the texts of Shakespeare if people are illiterate or if drama is a forgotten art? What happens to traditions of freedom, justice and democracy if people are not vigilant for them, or if lawyers, civil servants and politicians are uneducated or corrupt? What future has a Church that does not constantly study, nurture and improvise creatively upon its scriptures, traditions and worship?

Perhaps the most moving and generative open secrets in communities are those which unite suffering and celebration. I remember the first time I visited the L'Arche community for the severely handicapped at Trosly-Breuil in Northern France. It had been founded when Jean Vanier and a priest friend took two severely handicapped people to live with them there, and now there are 106 communities worldwide. I was one of a group of theologians from France and Britain who were invited to try to articulate what the meaning of L'Arche is. In a society that increasingly prefers to abort the handicapped, L'Arche stands for the utter preciousness of each person, whether handicapped or helper.

The handicapped raise issues of secrets and disciplines acutely. For some they are a shameful secret who lead to embarrassment and therefore need to be kept out of sight as much as possible. In Trosly at first there was considerable opposition to having a lot of handicapped in the village, and that has been repeated elsewhere. But there is a 'good secret' too. They are people who have a different experience of life, often very painful. Yet many of those in L'Arche cannot communicate well in words. Some have badly damaged brains. How can they share their secrets? How can they be part of the Christian or other faith community (there are L'Arche communities in Muslim, Hindu and multi-faith regions)? How can the image of God be discerned in them?

The question of disciplines is also acute. There are the demanding disciplines of the practical running of the community and the hard work and dedication needed to do that. But I was intrigued too by distinctive practices which had developed. The most obvious was the way in which bodies were so important to communication and building up the community. The interaction of faces was fascinating – so much was shared by looks, glances, frequent smiles and laughter. It was as if a new sort of beauty was appearing in both helpers and handicapped, as practices of appreciation and encouragement became habitual. One long-term helper from the Lambeth L'Arche in London, Katharine Hall, spoke of 'waiting for the beauty' in each person. It may take years and you may have to have your eyes opened to a new sort of beauty, but, she said, it appears, time and time again – and always differently.

The interaction of faces is only part of this, however. Touching is even more basic. It flows through the day – dressing, eating, carrying, hair care, bathing, playing, and just literally keeping in touch. Above all what struck me was its gentleness. The violence of our times is horrendous – physical violence, verbal violence, economic violence, institutional violence, spiritual violence. It is intensified by being vividly presented in the media, so that violence often dominates imaginations as well as behaviour. Yet here at L'Arche was a practice of touching, of handling people, which seemed like a prophetic sign of an alternative. It had enabled gentleness to be at the heart of this community.

This was not anything sentimental. There could be appropriate firmness or even toughness. Violence is a threat in L'Arche too. Jean Vanier talked about one experience: 'The screams of anguish awakened great violence in me. Because I was in community I was held. But parents of the disabled are frequently alone.' Helpers and handicapped are tested to their limits, and it is clear that for gentleness to survive it has to be sustained by a whole ecology of beliefs, practices and supports. At L'Arche the central practice is worship. There are regular Eucharists in which the disabled play a full role. In each household there is also singing together every day, with all sorts of participation, from enthusiastic joining in the singing to following the rhythm with whatever parts of the body can be moved.

All these regular disciplines in the service of the handicapped have their testing and their fulfilment in facing the overwhelming mystery of death. 'We are familiar with death here,' said Jean Vanier when I first went to Trosly. Visiting again two years later, in the household I was attached to Antonio was dying. I spent some time by his bedside as he lay hooked up to drips, his birthday presents piled on the bed. Life went on as usual in the household around him, and yet it was clear that Antonio had not long to live. This was realistically faced, but at the same time life in Antonio's presence seemed more vibrant. Jean said of him: 'It is beautiful but dangerous to live with him: he demands a lot of presence.' He was being given that presence, and the result was a dying that seemed like the fulfilment of a vocation.

So much in our Western culture fears death, denies it, represses it, sees it as the opposite of life and the worst that can happen to anyone. Many people regard severe disability as something like a living death, and so it shares something of death's unacceptability and disgrace. Disability, like death, gives a different perspective on many of the idols of our culture: success, comfort, health, being in control, sex, power. So part of the provocative witness of L'Arche is its following Jesus by living vibrantly in the face of death. The household sang daily as Antonio lay there. He regularly took communion. The way of Jesus to crucifixion and resurrection enabled facing death and disability in a certain spirit, blending utter realism with hope and joy. The overall effect was that death as an impersonal, irresistible, fearsome force was denied. Instead, there was no doubt what was the central reality: it was Antonio's remarkable face, with large, deep brown eyes – the awaited beauty.

THE DISCIPLINE OF THE SECRET AND THE SHARING OF THE MYSTERY OF GOD

In the early Church there was something called the *disciplina arcani*, the 'discipline of the secret'. Those who were not yet baptized but were being instructed in Christian faith were allowed to take part in the first part of the Eucharist when there are Bible readings, prayers and a sermon. But they had to withdraw for the actual communion: this was seen as a secret or mystery to be attended only by those who had been through instruction and baptism. In most of today's churches this is continued in requiring at least baptism of those who wish to participate in the bread and wine. The principle is that the mystery of Holy Communion requires appropriate disciplines.

I have been suggesting in this chapter that every good secret needs its disciplines. There is a proper role for boundaries and reserve about the things that go deepest and mean most to us. But there is another vital principle which must be observed if the relationship of secrets and disciplines is not to go wrong. This is that the secret must have priority over the discipline. The discipline must serve the secret and be appropriate to the secret. The world is full of disciplines which have lost their vital connections with the good secrets they are supposed to serve. We are familiar with over-secretive bureaucracies, secret services which undermine civil liberties, and professions which monopolize expertise in order to increase their own wealth and power.

In the Church the central mystery of the good news of God requires intimacy and the disciplines of intimacy. I have discussed some of the intimate and community forms of discipline. The Christian community's form of intimacy is symbolized by those committed in baptism coming together for Holy Communion. But the mystery of the Gospel also requires worldwide sharing, the communication of an unlimited invitation. There is in this open secret a dynamic uniting radical intimacy with widespread publicity. Both can go terribly and tragically wrong. Both require rigorous disciplines, and innovation in disciplines, if they are to be served well. But, as the example of Antonio in L'Arche has already suggested, there is one ultimate discipline at the heart of both.

This is the discipline of dying. The death of Jesus Christ is central to the Gospel and the Eucharist, and participation in baptism initiates Christians into this. Dying is also inseparable from the widespread communication of the Gospel. Martyrdom to the point of death is the ultimate discipline in witnessing to Jesus Christ, but it will be experienced in less drastic (though sometimes more humiliating) forms by anyone trying to conform their life and communication to the crucified Jesus Christ. So this is a mystery which pivots around death.

Yet there is an even deeper mystery. Death does not have the last word: God does. Death itself is overwhelmed in resurrection and is transformed in the process. Everything leads back and forwards to the mystery of God. In the topic of every chapter of this book the same theme surfaces. All the disciplines of Christian living – in intimacy and in community, in communication, action and suffering – go wrong if they are not serving the mystery of God. And religion is extraordinarily resourceful at disconnecting its rituals and practices from the living God. When this happens the disciplines end up serving idols.

It is therefore vital that witness to the mystery of God be renewed again and again. Christian history is full of reinvigorations, renewals, reformations, revivals and reconstitutions. Whenever that really happens the disciplines too are renewed – as in praying, meditating, community living, pilgrimage, charitable giving, singing, artistic creativity, studying, silence, smiling, gentleness and the art of dying well. But these are only true to the mystery if they find themselves constantly overwhelmed by it, as every fresh attempt to do justice to it ends in Paul's exclamation: 'Who is sufficient?'

FIVE

LEISURE AND WORK – SHAPING TIME AND ENERGY

'Rest before work' is the motto of a friend of mine. He does not see rest only as a reward for work already done. He takes time off before a specially busy period and just enjoys himself. He treats his day the same way, punctuating it with breaks for exercise or something leisurely. It is an energizing routine, and he gets a great deal done. Above all it breaks the power of one of the main compulsions of our society, addiction to urgency.

This addiction dominates the day with a string of urgent matters. It is deeply suspicious of rest or leisure so long as anything considered urgent remains to be done. We know we are suffering from it if, whenever we do one thing, we immediately think of ten more that need to be done and start doing one of them. In extreme cases it fills day after day with work, and the time for a break or a holiday never comes. In the worst instances of all, the addict combines with others to create a climate or culture of urgency in which nobody can take time off with an easy conscience. This and other distortions of the relation of leisure to work are common in a society whose main criterion for its own health is economic success, and which encourages people to focus their identities through their jobs. It means that facing up to issues about leisure and work, money, organizational life and the way our time is divided is – urgent! But first let us take a poetry break.

LEISURE

Here is Micheal O'Siadhail's poem called 'Leisure':

What does it mean?
Suddenly, effortlessly, to touch the core.
Mostly in the glow of friends
but today just strolling the length of a city street.
Carnival moments.
The apple back on its tree
in a garden lost, a garden longed for.

I move among traders.
Stacks of aubergines, rows of tiger-lilies.
Rings of silver and cornelian.
A feast of action.
Crosslegged, an Indian plays
music on a saw-blade glittering in the sun.

In the sweat of thy face
shalt thou eat bread. First hearing
that story, I'd bled for Adam.
I bump into an acquaintance and begin to apologize.
'Taking a break,
be hard at it tomorrow.'
Puritan me, so afraid of paradise.

Anaxagoras the sage
(a century before Plato) mulled it over
on a street like this in Athens.
First question: *Why are you here on earth?*

Answer: *To behold.*
No excuses called for.
Contemplation. Seeing. Fierce and intense.

This majesty. This fullness.
Does it all foreshadow another Eden?
The air is laden with yearning.
I can't say for what and I can't be silent either.
Rejoice. Rejoice.
To attest the gift of a day.
To saunter and gaze. To own the world.[1]

O'Siadhail interweaves the two main pictures of leisure and work that have fed into Western civilization. First there is the Genesis story of the garden of Eden. In the first creation story in Genesis chapter 1, the message seems to be: rest before work! Human beings are created on the sixth day, so their first full day alive is the seventh, the Sabbath on which God rested. We are created to rest first – in company with God. In Genesis chapter 2 the garden of Eden itself is to be cultivated and cared for: there is horticultural work in paradise. So the Genesis picture is of rest and leisure combined with creative and physical work. The invitation to 'be fruitful and multiply' suggests both sides – good sex flourishes where there can be leisure, celebration and sleep; but the life of any couple – even more when children multiply – calls for home-making, food provision and other labours.

The second picture is Greek, where the highest activity is contemplation and the gardening is left largely to slaves. There are tensions between the Hebrew and Greek which still run deep in our culture – we find strands which despise physical labour, which place the intellectual above the manual, or, in religious terms, value 'sacred' prayer and contemplation above 'secular' practical occupations. Against those, others see all honest work as pleasing God, with secular employment as potentially part of a vocation.

But O'Siadhail reaches deeper than these tensions to glimpse how Eden's paradise can be united with amazed appreciation of the world. The Hebrew and the Greek pictures both allow us to 'touch the core', to enjoy 'carnival moments', to 'saunter and gaze'. They both encourage us to be overwhelmed by something good, beautiful and enjoyable. The contemplative moment in Genesis is when 'God saw everything he had made, and behold, it was very good' (Genesis 1:31). Intense seeing is participation in the activity of a God who sees.

But what has gone wrong? The middle verse of the poem faces the distortion of work. There is an urge to apologize for enjoying life. We see ourselves as accountable before an ethic that views work alone as virtuous. This replaces accountability before a God who wants us to rest and enjoy as well as work.

SABBATICAL TIME

It is a liberation to believe that rest and leisure are just as much an imperative as work. It also affects the whole shape of our life. I remember a rabbi in a television interview being asked: 'How have the Jews managed to preserve the sabbath over thousands of years?' His reply was: 'It is not the Jews who have preserved the sabbath. The sabbath has preserved the Jews.'

There is a remarkable passage about the sabbath in Donald Nicholl's journal written while he was living in Jerusalem:

Nearly all our visitors who come to stay with us for any length of time eventually ask the same question: 'How on earth do people manage to remain sane in the midst of all the tension and craziness of this place?'

To this question there are many answers: such, for instance, as the shining example of all the holy people in our tension-ridden city. One day I hope to write about them. But there is an even simpler answer which, sadly, is beyond the experience of almost everyone outside Israel. I am speaking of the Sabbath. Of the Sabbath it is eminently true to say, 'Taste and see that it is good,' for unless you taste it you cannot appreciate its goodness.

And you taste it in the most unlikely places. After all, Netanya is a Mediterranean holiday centre where you would expect to encounter the usual noise of the modern entertainment world – anything but the quiet of the Sabbath. Yet when we arrived there at lunchtime on Friday, you could already feel the town settling steadily into the silence of the holy day. The volume of traffic had gradually diminished: the shops were closing their doors; and even the pedestrians were beginning to move more slowly, their voices quieter as they greeted one another, '*Shabbat Shalom*'. By the time the sun was setting over the Mediterranean the beach was unpeopled and those of us sitting on benches or strolling along the tree-lined sea front were beginning to breathe more unhurriedly, scenting the fragrance of *Shabbat*.

When I looked up towards the hotel where we were staying, there, to my joy, I saw that the common room was now lit up and filled with my Jewish fellow guests dressed in their prayer shawls and wearing their yarmulkas. At that moment it seemed completely right and proper for them to be davening [a form of prayer characterized by swaying of the body] on behalf of those of us outside – except that I did not feel to be outside, because I was being embraced within the light to lighten the Gentiles.

A strange thought then entered my head: how I wish that the spiritually starving youngsters from Liverpool, Newcastle, Stoke and other cities might taste the sweetness of the Sabbath! Because then they might again see goodness. But England no longer knows 'the mystery of the Sabbath ... the table wreathed with precious mystery. Deep and hidden, beyond the reach of the word.' So her hungry children never taste Sabbath and cannot, therefore, see goodness.[2]

Like O'Siadhail, Nicholl makes the connection of right leisure and rest with full seeing, but this is now taken further to embrace goodness. Can it really be so vital to breathe in 'the fragrance of *Shabbat*'? Nicholl calls it a mystery; the previous chapter explored this in terms of a secret with its own discipline. It is 'the gift of a day', and part of the discipline is simply to receive it. The temptation is to say things like: 'But I have not finished my work'; 'I do not deserve a day off this week'; 'Look at what could be achieved by using the time differently'; 'Am I not being legalistic?'; 'Should I be different from so many others?'; 'My family won't survive if I do not work in all the time available.' There are dozens of other temptations not to welcome this day, to refuse the invitation just to celebrate it. The attitude of obedience to the Sabbath command is a good way of avoiding getting entangled in the temptations, setting them to one side in order to get on with the essential matter of breathing the fragrance, tasting and seeing.

It need not be blind obedience – occasionally it is irresponsible to refuse to work on the sabbath. But to take a free, responsible decision to work while really desiring to celebrate the sabbath is very different from the same decision made without remembering the taste. The heart of the matter is the savour of leisure that is desired by God and invites us to trust God more fully. A little later in his journal Nicholl, in an aside, gives a Muslim example: 'It was Sunday morning and our skilful handyman, Yakoub, was sitting on his porch drinking coffee with that air of leisured satisfaction which in itself is already a vote of confidence in God...'

What happens when the wisdom of the sabbath wins us over and starts to shape our life? I am not interested in saying just how the sabbath should be observed – clearly both Jews and Christians have a wide variety of ways of honouring it, and most Christians have even changed the day from Saturday to Sunday. But however it is observed, there are profound effects when, every week, this radical discontinuity happens in the interests of God, celebration and rest. It has the potential to transform the ecology of our time and energy. It sets the tone for the week. It is like an optics which lets us see the week in proper perspective. It can change our view of what is worth working for the rest of the week. Many of the 'practices of excess' discussed in the previous chapter can have more scope on the sabbath. It attests something unnecessary, excessive, superfluous, superabundant. If we do not have a 'container' view of time (which sees time as a neutral medium unaffected by what goes on in it), but instead see time being shaped by its contents, then time itself is affected by this celebration and freedom from work.

This wisdom spreads to affect larger and smaller units of time than the week. We can have little sabbaths in the day: spaces when we can pause, rest, enjoy, recollect, be quiet; savour a sight, taste, sound, thought or person – 'no excuses called for'. We can have larger sabbaths in the year: holidays, retreats, breaks of many sorts. An increasing number of jobs offer the possibility of sabbatical leave. In the Bible the principle is extended to the land:

'in the seventh year there shall be a sabbath of solemn rest for the land, a sabbath to the Lord' (Leviticus 25:4). And after seven times seven years the fiftieth is a jubilee year, when land is returned to its original owners, slaves set free and debts remitted. It may be that this pattern was never actually followed by Israel, but its message is clear: the rhythms of time in work and rest are of immense importance for life.

What are the effects of this 'free' sabbatical time in the day, the week, the year, the career, and the long-term cycles of community life? Negatively, it helps to break the hold of powerful compulsions. These are bound up with some of our strongest urges: to survive, to prosper, to have money, to exercise our gifts, to deal with problems, to be successful, to be productive, to contribute to the community, to have recognition and status. None of these are wrong, but just because they are so basic and good they can become idols, absorbing all our time and energy. The sabbath interrupts this idolatry, and challenges whatever other than God that threatens to dominate our time.

Positively, it opens the way for the creative shaping of time. The church year is the main Christian example of a still continuing creativity which has been exercised century after century in developing a habitable pattern of time. It is punctuated by sabbaths, feasts and fasts. Endless variations and improvisations on it are possible by individuals and traditions. These constructive reshapings of time are especially desirable in a period like ours, when there is widespread disruption and confusion of time patterns. The guiding principle is simple: we are created first to enjoy God and creation at leisure, and unless special times are devoted to this we will be trapped in unhealthy compulsions and idolatries.

THE OVERWHELMING WORLD OF WORK

If our vocation (or calling) is, as chapter 2 suggested, to desire God and what God desires, then our work cannot be the whole of our vocation. We are called to do other things besides work. But clearly work is required. God is described as working, and also inviting people to participate in what is to be done. To be productive, to help shape the world and to take responsibility for managing resources is not just an economic necessity but is a way of fulfilling the desires of God and living 'in the image of God'.

If God is intimately involved in the whole of creation – energizing it, judging it and affirming it – then the world of work must be thought of as being shaped by God, and any split between the religious and the secular should be resisted. One of the most damaging splits is between, on the one side, a religious life which goes on in a separate sphere, and, on the other, the practical activities that take up most of our time and energy. The Protestant Reformation made a prophetic stand on this and insisted that God calls people into ordinary, worldly occupations as service to God that is as valuable as any other. Recent Roman Catholic social teaching has also been strong on this. But how to overcome the split today requires fresh effort to understand the world of work and the profound changes that have been happening in it.

The scale of human work is vast. Scarcely a part of the natural world is left untouched. Massive continuing transformations are achieved. Nature is integrated into a 'second nature' – towns and cities, homes and schools, transport and communications, agriculture and fishing, manufacture and business, politics and law, armies and hospitals, science and technology, and the billions of daily transactions that make up global civilization. Work sustains and develops all this.

The dynamics of this 'second nature' are becoming more complex and intensive. Let us take just a few changes that affect most of us in some form and have a special impact on our economic activities. They are some of the characteristic over-whelmings of our times.

A global economy

The global economy is the most obvious reality. Workers in different continents are directly in competition with each other. Corporations which are bigger than many national economies transfer contracts around the world, and not even long-established large workplaces feel safe. The financial markets mirror and intensify this globalization, as capital shifts rapidly and immense sums of money are transferred daily. There is an unprecedented volume of exchanges of goods, services, people, knowledge and information.

The global marketplace produces many casualties. There are the unemployed and also those who are constantly overworked. There are communities, nations and even global regions which are not 'successful' – about thirty million people a year die of starvation alone. Only a minority of the world's population are considered well off, and even among them many are under extreme economic pressures. Debt is probably the single most oppressive economic reality for nations, organizations, families and individuals. Its weight radically affects the shape of living and, in open or hidden ways, dictates fundamental decisions about time and energy. The environment is often another casualty of economic activity, with the rich damaging it more than the poor. Yet there is a credit side to the balance sheet too, under headings such as the benefits for many people of prosperity, education, access to culture, health, democracy, new patterns of organization and management, and a range of constructive ways of coping with the problems of the new economic dynamics.

Information revolution and knowledge explosion

A second massive development, closely linked to the first, is the information revolution. In a very short time information technology has spanned the world. This affects the nature of work and the rest of life for vast numbers of people. The typical result of the industrial revolution was to synchronize work closely with machines. This is intensified, and a whole new type of work is created, when the machines are mainly to do with information, knowledge and communication networks. These have spread across the labour economy: computers, information systems, cellular communications networks, machines with 'artificial intelligence' doing a wide range of manufacturing tasks, electronic imaging, cybernetic quality control, complex financial modelling, and simulation of almost every scenario of the future.

Where is the 'workplace' if we can be hooked up at home? What happens to the 'working day' if we can log in at any time of the day or night, and store what we have done for use at another time? The boundaries between work and home, work and leisure, are complexified. But more profoundly our identity as workers is transformed by being part of this network. It sets us in the midst of an overwhelming number of potential relationships with people and sources of information.

The information revolution also means that we as workers are the most recorded, scanned and screened in history. Think of our financial records and credit ratings, medical and genetic information, educational and employment history, taxation, driving and criminal records, security clearance, advertising and political surveys, and more.

The information revolution has accompanied an unprecedented explosion of knowledge and techniques. An increasing number of jobs are knowledge-based, and workers have to learn throughout their lives. I once met an employee of a computer company who reckoned that he had to assimilate the equivalent of a three-year university degree every four years in order to keep up with his speciality. The combination of information technology with rapid developments in knowledge and techniques is a new overwhelming with which millions of people cope daily.

This can be intoxicating and inspiring, as one wave of innovation follows another. Challenges and possibilities multiply. But there is another side of it. Even forgetting the many who are excluded from the information and knowledge culture, a large percentage of those included have boring jobs doing routine work in front of screens. Either way, the new development is the extent to which human beings become 'operators', integrated into systems which always threaten to take them over, and whose long-term consequences are unknown.

Everything a commodity

A third overwhelming development turns more and more things and aspects of life into commodities with a price attached. Money becomes more pervasive in relation to health, education, culture, and almost any service or use of time which is to the benefit of someone else. It comes as a shock at first to find that the friendly advice given by a solicitor is being timed and billed. And our priest next? Nothing is immune to having its monetary value assessed: for good commercial reasons, McDonalds counter staff are told to smile at customers and look them in the eye.

What is happening here? 'Commodification' of everything often has a sensible, realistic basis: after all, even priests need money to live. It is often hard to draw lines between what we all agree has to be priced and what we find harder to see in money terms. Part of the definition of work is that it is about exchanges of goods and services that people consider valuable, and money is rightly seen as a key way of measuring value.

The problem is not so much the importance of money. The key question is how it relates to other important things in the dynamic exchanges that shape our lives. Is money 'the bottom line'? The image of a bottom line on a piece of paper or set of accounts is flat and two-dimensional. In fact there are many sides of life, and each side has its bottom line. Multi-dimensional overwhelming – by people, desires, beauty, truth, goodness, mysteries, suffering and joy as well as money – means that we have to seek wisdom in how to relate many bottom lines. Our shape of life has to do justice to the whole ecology. Commodification is dangerous when money is the only bottom line.

****

So work is of immense importance in shaping our world and our lives, and the global market, the information revolution and knowledge explosion, and seeing everything in terms of money, are just some examples of new dimensions of work today which intensify its capacity to overwhelm us. But coping with all this cannot be confined to solutions within the sphere of work: it will crucially depend on the interaction between spheres. How is our work to be shaped in the midst of multiple overwhelmings?

THE NETWORK OF EXCHANGES

Work is part of the dynamic network of exchanges which shape life – we have just been looking at exchanges that involve goods, services, energy, money, knowledge and information. Previous chapters have discussed some of the other types of exchange: in relating to those important to us, in promising, in good and bad behaviour, in communication, in prayer and worship. It is no accident that religion, sex and money, those topics which English 'good manners' suggest that it is most dangerous to raise in polite company, are all about exchanges that can go powerfully right or wrong.

Our identity is made up of such exchanges and the patterns they form. If there are major changes in any of them our sense of self is threatened. If our work pattern changes, as in the shift from a job to being unemployed (or better, being unwaged – the unemployed are often under stronger pressure to do a great many time-consuming things just to get by, and so are not by any means 'out of work'), then it does not just affect our income. Often, a job is also a social network, it gives status, it allows us to contribute to society in some way, it lets us have the satisfaction of achieving something, and is important for our self-esteem. To lose all that is a massive blow and throws us back on other patterns of exchange in ways that often produce crises in them too – unemployment increases the danger of divorce and of a general loss of meaning, purpose and sense of worth. But of course the dynamics of the exchanges can go terribly wrong for people with jobs too, not least because we can become addicted to work and its urgencies.

So all of us – not least for the sake of the better shaping of work, whether in paid employment or not – need to seek wisdom about the exchanges we take part in. For the rest of this chapter I want to focus on three of the many areas where wisdom is needed: the great exchange of the work of God in the world; the patterning of exchanges in organizations and institutions; and the management of our time.

THE GREAT EXCHANGE

I remember the excitement of being given a key insight when working with Frances Young on our book on Paul's Second Letter to the Corinthians. My father-in-law, Daniel Hardy, suggested that the economics of the letter be examined. What seemed like a strange idea proved extraordinarily fruitful, and continues to be so.

At the heart of it is the conception of God, whose created world is the work in which all human work participates. And God has done something in Jesus Christ which has produced a resource that Paul compares to creation – a new creation. He is overwhelmed by it, and it draws him into being one of God's 'co-workers' (2 Corinthians 6:1). Just as, in the Genesis story, there is first sabbath then work, so here there is gift followed by gratitude-inspired work. The gift is described as itself an exchange. A key Greek term is *katallagé* (5:18). This originally meant the exchange of money, a money-lender's profit, or merchandise. It then came to mean the exchange of enmity for friendship, and so 'reconciliation'. Paul sees God reconciling people through Christ,

121

and making himself, Paul, a *diakonos* (minister, meaning a slave who waited at table and did other forms of manual work) of reconciliation, whose content is this crucial exchange:

> For the love of Christ urges us on, because we are convinced that one has died for all; therefore all have died. And he died for all, so that those who live might live no longer for themselves, but for him who died and was raised for them ... For our sake he made him to be sin who knew no sin, so that in him we might become the righteousness of God. (2 Corinthians 5:14,15,21)

This is an exchange that generates further exchanges, setting in motion a chain reaction of love, sacrifice and communication. This is life 'in the Spirit', and the first chapter of 2 Corinthians is one of the most powerful testimonies to its quality of expansive interchange which embraces God, human beings and the most intractable realities of suffering and death. Jesus Christ gave himself in exchange for new life for others. To have his Spirit (a 'down-payment' – 1:22) is to be freed to spend ourselves in new ways for God and others. It is also to have a radically different criterion by which to judge our lives. Paul later describes in the language of measuring scales the ultimate perspective of his 'exchange rate mechanism':

> For our light, momentary affliction (this slight distress of the passing hour) is ever more and more abundantly preparing *and* producing *and* achieving for us an everlasting weight of glory [beyond all measure, excessively surpassing all comparisons and all calculations, a vast and transcendent glory and blessedness never to cease!]. (2 Corinthians 4:17; Amplified Bible)

That underlines a key thing: this 'economy of God' is one of limitless abundance. The basic fact is 'the extraordinary (surpassing) power of God' (4:7), 'the extraordinary (surpassing) grace of God' (9:14). It overflows in many ways, with 'grace abounding to more and more people' as the mark of God's and Paul's work. It culminates in Paul's 'exultation' in chapters 10–12. There Paul tells how the strange exchange of the crucifixion was brought home to him in the most intimate way. He was suffering from an unspecified 'thorn in the flesh':

> Three times I appealed to the Lord about this, that it would leave me, but he said to me, 'My grace [loving-kindness, mercy] is sufficient for you, for power is made perfect in weakness.' So I will glory all the more gladly in my weaknesses, so that the power of Christ may dwell in me. Therefore I am content with weaknesses, insults, hardships, persecutions, and calamities for the sake of Christ, for whenever I am weak, then I am strong. (2 Corinthians 12:8–10)

But a key question now is how this abundance of God connects with actual finances. This leads into one of the most remarkable economic statements in the New Testament, in 2 Corinthians chapters 8–9.

In these chapters Paul writes about the collection of money he is making for the poor of the church in Jerusalem and urges the Corinthians to contribute. He praises the Macedonians as full participants in the economy of God:

> for, during a severe ordeal of affliction, their abundant joy and their extreme poverty have overflowed in a wealth of generosity on their part. For, as I can testify, they voluntarily gave

according to their means, and even beyond their means.
(2 Corinthians 8:2–3)

I was often reminded of that during fifteen years living in inner-city Birmingham, seeing there a higher level of giving, proportionate to income, than in the suburbs.

But Paul is also realistic and does not tell the Corinthians to risk poverty. All he asks is that they see that, before God, economics is basically about sharing, meeting needs and looking to the common good:

For there is no intention that relief for others should bring affliction to you; but for the present time, on the basis of equality, your overflow should make up their shortage, so that their overflow may make up your shortage, that equality may prevail. (2 Corinthians 8:13–14)

That is clearly the minimal response to God's generosity. It is in line with much teaching about fair distribution in Judaism and in Greek ethics. But Paul puts it into a context that opens up this minimum to continual expansion. How he does this is of immense significance.

His basic move is to redescribe the heart of the Gospel in terms of money and exchange:

For you know the grace [generous act] of our Lord Jesus Christ, that though he was rich, yet for your sakes he became poor, so that by his poverty you might become rich. (2 Corinthians 8:9)

This is in line with the God who 'loves a cheerful giver' and is described, in the culmination in chapter 9:7–15, in terms of overwhelming generosity, setting off a chain of interchange in money, blessings, prayer and gratitude.

That remarkable passage interweaves the 'material' and the 'spiritual' so as to make them inseparable in the light of Jesus Christ. As Frances Young and I worked on these two chapters, we were astonished at the way in which Paul's use of Greek makes this point again and again. One major New Testament scholar, Nils Dahl, even says that Paul here expresses himself 'in a way which is impossible to translate'. It is because Paul is using one key word in his Gospel after another to refer to the collection – grace, fellowship/participation, service, blessing, generosity, abundance/overflow, and others.

What is happening? Paul is both interpreting the Gospel in terms of money and at the same time transforming attitudes to money through the Gospel. He is stretching language to do justice to a radical vision of how deeply God is concerned with money and how it can be a means of exchanges which transform life. If we soak in the message of these chapters our practice of faith and our financial transactions could not stay the same.

What about work? Throughout this Paul assumes that hard work is the norm. This is so for him in his life of tent-making and building up churches; for the Macedonians, who in their poverty are almost certain to have earned through manual labour what they gave away; and for the Corinthians, who also, as evidence from the New Testament and elsewhere makes clear, mostly earned their living with their hands.

In today's world too the majority of Christians do not live in affluent circumstances but are immersed in harsh economic reality – most live in the less prosperous southern hemisphere. The poverty of Jesus in his itinerant ministry is well known. Less well recognized is the reality behind Paul's insistence on working at making tents for his living rather than depending on gifts from Christians. What this meant for him is described vividly by the scholar Ronald Hock in a thorough historical study:

> More than any of us has supposed, Paul was *Paul the Tent-maker*. His trade occupied much of his time – from the years of his apprenticeship through the years of his life as a missionary of Christ, from before daylight through most of the day. Consequently, his trade in large measure determined his daily experiences and his social status. His life was very much that of the workshop – of artisan friends like Aquila, Barnabas and perhaps Jason; of leather, knives and awls; of wearying toil; of being bent over a workbench like a slave and of working side by side with slaves; of thereby being perceived by others and by himself as slavish and humiliated, of suffering the artisan's lack of status and so being reviled and abused.[4]

So Paul wrote about money and generosity from within that work situation. The result is a model of coping with multiple overwhelmings, in which money and work are decisively 'baptized' in the reality of Jesus Christ's pivotal exchange.

OUR NETWORK OF MEMBERSHIP

G.K. Chesterton remarked that when people are at their most lively, inspired and creative one of the things they habitually do is to create institutions. This was certainly true of Paul. Besides tent-making his work was founding and building up the first urban churches. In collaboration with others he was organizing, networking, shaping patterns of worship and other community behaviour, tackling problems of authority, status, money and rival conceptions of the Church, and negotiating relations with other groups and institutions. If an 'institution' is understood as an organized group that endures over time, then Paul was engaged in forming and maintaining an institution.

He and his collaborators were remarkably creative in this. They drew on the wisdom of Israel above all – centuries of experience of a covenant community which had led in their own time to the synagogue, with its worship, ethics and politics, shaped by traditions of law, history, wisdom, poetry and prophecy. But they also learnt from the two main institutions of the Roman Empire, the state, including the law courts, and the household, which was also the economic unit where most productive work was done. The result was a complex, new sort of community which has been much studied recently by scholars of the sociology and social history of early Christianity.[5]

Down the centuries similar institutional creativity has been practised century after century in the Church. It is common today to despise the 'institutional church', but without having long-term organization and structures it would not be there at all. That has involved generations of people putting thought, time and energy into building it up, raising money, taking part in debates and conflicts, and at times reforming it.

I remember taking part at Swanwick in a conference of lay people from the Church of England Diocese of Sheffield. Most parishes were represented, and each had a display about what they were doing. Besides worship, prayer, pastoral work and building maintenance, they embraced hundreds of groups focused on activities from prison visiting, crèches and community organizing to drama, music and brewing. I met some of the people who were responsible for creating and sustaining all this year after year, in a diocese with a high proportion of poorer parishes. I thought what a privilege it was: these presentations and these people are usually invisible to the rest of the world, scattered in places the media are not interested in, but here they were, gathered in one place. Then I multiplied it to imagine ordinary, largely hidden and unsensational Christianity around the world, probably over one and a half billion people taking part in millions of closer or looser organizations. And each group and institution requires, if it is to flourish, people who work at founding and sustaining it.

Is this not one of the most underrated forms of work? Who wants to be secretary or treasurer or on the committee? Who wants to examine budgets, raise funds or do the correspondence? Who wants to think up policy and persuade others? Some always do; but more people probably take these things on as work necessary to serve fellow members and the locality. As Lesslie Newbigin has said, God can be glorified by committees too!

It is similar in other institutions besides the Church. An immense amount of time and energy goes into other religious communities and into businesses, schools, universities, clubs, learned and other societies, armies, civil services, hospitals, professional groups, trades unions, political parties, legal systems, theatres, broadcasting organizations, and – perhaps most fundamental of all – families. Each of those is involved in the complex exchanges of society, and one of the main forms of work is managing them. Any one of them can be all-consuming, its urgencies taking over members' lives. All of them require a flow of wisdom and discernment if they are to flourish.

This is not the place to go further into that wisdom, much of which has to be specific to one institution in its particular time, place and purposes. But the conclusion for the shape of living is that, just as each of us has a 'community of the heart' made up of the most significant people in our lives, so we are part of a 'network of membership' in institutions. We find ourselves in some institutions without any, or much, choice; others we join voluntarily. All require work if they are to be begun and sustained, and part of our vision of life should be found in answering questions such as the following.

Is our main Christian vocation in work to be carried out largely in church institutional activities or in a business, a home, a trade union, manual work, a political party, or some other 'secular' sphere?

What should our balance of institutional commitments be?

How can our particular gifts help to build up, and if necessary reform, worthwhile institutions? How might our institutional creativity and service be developed?

How do the various institutions to which we belong relate to God's purposes of peace, justice, freedom, goodness, truth and love?

How might we show gratitude to God for institutions and those who work for them, and pray for them faithfully?

SHAPING TIME

How we spend time reveals, more than most indicators, how our life is being shaped through the multiple exchanges of leisure and work. I suspect that it is not just our tendency to dramatize ourselves which makes us feel that our own culture has special problems with time.

Competition for our time in a culture of distraction

We live in a 'culture of distraction'. On its leisure side, this means an inundation of entertainment. Probably nothing has changed the atmosphere of public and private life more than the past forty or so years of mass entertainment. Mass communications – print, radio, terrestrial and satellite television, cinema, video, tape, records and computers – have shaped a very different culture from anything previous generations have been exposed to. Traumatic violence and intimate sexual scenes are routine experiences, and it is possible to have non-stop sport, news, films, pornography, music, games, 'soaps', and so on.

On its 'work' side the economic pressures towards greater efficiency and productivity have meant that more is demanded of workers. This often includes more varied tasks, tighter deadlines and stricter accountability for time, together with a great deal of new learning on the job. This 'drives people to distraction' by multiple demands and responsibilities, and success often means that the pay is increased but the demands are intensified. And over it all there is often the anxiety of a short-term contract or simply the lack of any job security.

In the midst of all this we try to cope with a fragmentation of, and often competition between, the rhythms of time by which we live. The clocks and calendars by which we time our lives have never been more varied. My own life in the apparently peaceful tempo of Cambridge is a nodal point for diverse patterns of time, many of which pull in different directions. Like most people, I am involved with a range of institutions and groups. I work to timescales ranging from a deadline of yesterday through a week, a term, or a four-year project, to a lifetime, or the building up of an institution that might last many more centuries. My work goes on not only in lecture rooms, committee rooms, conferences and my office, but also at home – so boundaries are often blurred. Through it all are the rhythms of my biological clock to do with night and day, food, sleep and exercise, time of year and time of life. These are criss-crossed by the timescales and priorities of other people and their institutions, and by constant interruption by visitors, telephone calls, faxes, E-mails and traditional letters.

But if this feels distracted, I look at others. They work in financial markets dealing simultaneously with many institutions and dealers around the world and around the clock. They work night shifts, or in businesses struggling for survival against competition. They are junior doctors, or teachers in badly-run and under-funded schools, or free-lance journalists living day to day, or single parents of young children. Or they are unemployed, and have to do everything the least expensive way and keep some pattern in a day which no institution or job shapes.

Occupational rhythms, timescales and deadlines are themselves criss-crossed by others – the media have their schedules, so do friends, family members, and all the clubs, groups and organizations we belong to. There are wider patterns – a political party's time in power, economic cycles, fashions, even historical epochs; and as we approach the year 2000 we think back over millennia. In short, life takes time, but it is timed simultaneously in very different ways. So how, in the midst of conflicting demands, the threat of multiple distractions and the dissipation of time in many directions, is time to be shaped?

Time management

The idea of 'managing' our time suggests that we are in charge of it more than we are. Actually we are mostly passive. This is obvious in the big things, such as when we are born or die. But even in handling our own day, week or year we depend a great deal on other people and on events and decisions outside our control.

The first wisdom about time is therefore the virtue of patience. To be patient means that we recognize that everything cannot go according to our schedule and our desires. There is in life a great deal of waiting, postponement, delay and disappointment. Anyone with children knows that this is one of the basic lessons for them to learn and one of the hardest for us to teach – partly because as parents we spend a lot of energy being impatient with our children.

Impatience is not just about finding it hard to wait, it also tends to spoil time and relationships. Losing patience often changes for the worse the very thing we are wanting to happen. The birthday 'surprise' is not so good a week in advance, and also affects the birthday. Not being able to wait for sexual experience can do long-term damage. Not being able to wait for another person to share a secret in their own time can cut off or hurt a friendship. Groups and organizations too need patience if conflicts and destructive actions are to be avoided. Patience is an attitude to time which trusts that there is a 'right time' which is worth waiting for. Even if it never seems to come, is it better to do wrong, or to trust God in a future different from what we want?

A second piece of wisdom about time is what traditionally was called 'prudence', which literally means 'seeing ahead'. Prudence in that sense of foresight is not about being cautious and afraid to take risks. It is trying to look ahead and be prepared. This is quite a discipline, and it covers many of the things that time management experts teach millions of people every year. We need to make lists and arrange for reminders. We should try to anticipate difficulties, circumstances and reactions – our imaginations need to be exercised. Planning needs to be taken very seriously, and that includes deciding about priorities.

One of the gurus of time management, Stephen R. Covey, divides things to be done into four quadrants of a circle: urgent and important; not urgent and important; not urgent and not important; urgent and not important.[6] The key to the best time management is to develop the second quadrant, the important but not urgent. That is the one we are most tempted to neglect in the pressures of life. It includes the elements essential to foresight and preparation for a worthwhile future: planning, building relationships and trust, leisure that really refreshes and re-creates us, learning, training, and becoming clearer about our values and goals.

A third piece of wisdom is the habit of alertness, already discussed in chapter 2. If God is a God of abundance then each day is packed with possibilities. How often do we look back at a conversation or at a period of our life and say 'If only I'd noticed, if only I hadn't been so blind'? Alertness to opportunities goes with trust in a God who is richly active through what is happening. Even with the bad events we need to be always watching for God's way through them, bringing good out of them. There is always far more going on than we notice, so our attentiveness can never be too great. The abundant eventfulness of life is an overwhelming which is best met with constant alertness. If the Bible's encouragement to be alert, vigilant, watchful, and awake is put together with equally frequent encouragement not to be anxious and fearful, then we have a recipe for a heart and mind ready to discern the right shaping of time day by day.

The final wisdom comes back to the church year. It reminds us of the most basic truth of all about our time. Our time is God's time. We need to allow our time to be managed by God. That does not by any means take away our freedom. It rather gives us the freedom of a responsibility something like that of jazz musicians, who know what 'time' they are playing in and are for that very reason able to improvise and syncopate. The church year offers a ground bass for the rest of life.

THE DRAMA OF EUCHARISTIC TIME

To use a different picture, the church year gives us the plot of the big drama in which our life is a little role – each of us is one character who needs to recognize what he or she is part of. The climax of the church year is Easter, when the final drama of the life, death and resurrection of Jesus is celebrated. But that drama is also at the heart of the Lord's Supper, Holy Communion or Eucharist. So whenever we celebrate the Eucharist we identify with the drama afresh and see our own lives in its light. To do this week after week, year after year, can transform our sense of time past, present and future.

So the transformation is that we begin to live in eucharistic time, remembering, loving and hoping in Jesus Christ. As regards the past, remembering Jesus generates a double practice before God. The first practice is giving thanks for what was good. This makes the good of the past present to us again, and so lets it help shape the present and future. In gratitude there is an overflow of the goodness of the past towards the future. The second practice is lamenting what was bad and if necessary asking forgiveness for ourselves. This has the effect of refusing to repress the bad but also interrupting its power to shape the present and future.

As regards the present, eucharistic time reminds us of the 'real presence' of Jesus Christ. The fact that he gives himself to us afresh intensifies both our joy and our responsibility in each moment. His is the face before whom we are living now.

As regards the future, Jesus Christ embodies our hope – our ultimate judgement and joy will be before this face, so he is the criterion for all plans, prudence, urgency and importance.

The Eucharist can therefore become the basic shaper of our time and energy. Its context is the church year which draws us through the great acts of the drama of the Bible, and also reminds us, through stories and saints' days, of some of the main characters of the drama in biblical times and since. How can our own life be part of the present continuation of that drama? How can the schedules, calendars and urgencies of our families, jobs, leisure and other activities resonate with the rhythms and melodies of eucharistic time? How can we learn more of the wisdom and habits of patience, prudence and alertness? If the creation story in Genesis 1 is about God shaping time, with human beings made in that God's image, then one of the great challenges of human existence is here: how can we be shaped by God's time and respond by our own creative shaping of time?

THE MOMENT

William Blake in his poem *Milton* describes this creativity with time:

> But others of the Sons of Los build Moments & Minutes &
>   Hours
> And Days & Months & Years & Ages & Periods, wondrous
>   buildings;

And every Moment has a Couch of gold for soft repose.

Such a 'Moment' is seen as the pivot of each day:

> There is a Moment in each Day that Satan cannot find,
> Nor can his Witch Fiends find it; but the Industrious find
> This Moment and it multiply, and when it once is found
> It renovates every Moment of the Day if rightly placed.[7]

It is a vision of the 'industrious' finding a moment of 'repose' which can then energize and 'renovate' a whole day. Such a moment makes all our patience, prudence and alertness more than worthwhile. And 'moments' can renovate lives and periods as well as days. Their power of renewal is astonishing as they 'multiply' – just think of the conversion of Paul; or that 'moment' of the Last Supper, multiplied century after century!

Blake's final phrase, 'if rightly placed', suggests that we do not only passively wait for the moment. Rather, finding the moment is just the beginning of a continuing wisdom and creativity which constructs those 'wondrous buildings', the shape of our time in which rest and industriousness live together. This architecture of life in time is our home in the face of the many 'Witch Fiends' who threaten us with overwhelming urgencies, with dissipations of time and energy, and with the disruption of our gratitude and forgiveness for the past, our alertness to God in the present, and our patient hope for the future.

SIX

KNOCKED OUT OF SHAPE –
EVIL, SUFFERING AND DEATH

Suffering is the greatest teacher; the consecrated suffering of one soul teaches another. I think we have got all our values wrong, and suffering is the crown of life. Suffering and expansion, what a rich combination!

Religion has never made me happy; it's no use shutting the eyes to the fact that the deeper you go, the more alone you will find yourself. Suffering can expand, suffering can contract. *La souffrance noble, la souffrance basse.* Grasp the nettle, my little old thing! Religion has never made me comfy. I have been in the deserts ten years. All deepened life is deepened suffering, deepened dreariness, deepened joy. Suffering and joy. The final note of religion is joy.[1]

That sort of statement can only be made by someone who has 'been in the deserts ten years'. Even then its positive view of suffering is terribly dangerous. Most of us can think of people who are examples of the appalling fact that 'suffering can contract'. Worse than that, it can crush the joy and the life out of individuals and groups. We think of people who never recover from abuse, humiliation, torture, bereavement, depression or failure. There can be no romanticizing of suffering, no easy accounting for it as a stage on the way to joy. When we ourselves

137

suffer severely we become only too aware of the cliff edge we walk. Unless, somehow, we are held, we know we are in daily (and especially nightly) danger of falling into the abyss of despair, giving up in the face of this uncontrollable overwhelming. Perhaps as bad as despair, we may know the temptation of the sufferer to make others suffer too, so that the vicious spiral embraces more and more. There is an added twist to the agony when, as so often, the suffering is connected with malice, selfishness, indifference, injustice, or some other form of evil.

So how can we be held in our suffering? If, as von Hügel says, part of the experience is that we become more and more alone, that question is sharpened. Extreme suffering typically cuts us off from people, often from those who could best help us. It isolates us, drives us in on ourselves, makes us think that nobody could know what it is like. It can also, of course, unite us to them even more deeply, but that is not by any means an automatic process. The statistics of marriage break-up show it is more likely after losing a child. Many survivors of Auschwitz found it extremely difficult to resume 'normal' family life and friendships. Our deepest relationships are on the line in any situation of severe suffering. So how can we be held?

THE TESTIMONY OF SUFFERERS

Donald Nicholl in his Jerusalem journal tells of meeting

> a quiet, gentle man. He had about him an air which is quite unmistakable, the same air that I have virtually always sensed about men who survived the Japanese prison camps of the Second World War. Obviously you can't put your finger on it,

otherwise you would not have to describe it as 'an air'; but it is, indeed, unmistakable. The air about such men has something to do with their having gone further into suffering and the depths both of human cruelty and of fidelity than one ever imagined possible, yet having emerged still compassionate, gentle human beings. Such people are indelibly marked, as by a sacrament.

And he was one of those people. We learnt that he had spent years in Auschwitz and, on being liberated, was overwhelmed by the need to tell the story of Auschwitz and its victims. So after making his way to Tel Aviv he had straight away established himself in an abandoned concrete bunker and, like some hermit vowed to a secret cult, he had devoted himself night and day to describing the world of Auschwitz. When the books that he wrote appeared in print the Jewish reading public quickly recognized that here was someone truly inspired to give voice to their sufferings.[2]

I suppose most of us have a few such witnesses to great suffering in our 'community of the heart'. They hold us in our own suffering in a strange way, beyond the capacity of others who have not suffered like that. My own community of well-known sufferers includes Sheila Cassidy, who was tortured for giving medical treatment to a revolutionary in Chile, as told in her book *Audacity to Believe*. She went on to direct a hospice for the dying, and also to explore the themes of suffering, evil and death in *Sharing the Darkness* and *Good Friday People*. Other members are Dietrich Bonhoeffer, imprisoned and executed for plotting against Hitler; Alexander Solzhenitsyn, who wrote *The Gulag Archipelago* and several novels out of his years in Soviet labour camps; St Thérèse of Lisieux, who sustained years of spiritual desolation, culminating in a final illness during which physical degeneration combined with terrible doubt and threats to her sanity – she exclaimed at that time: 'I would never have believed it possible to suffer so much'; and Margaret Spufford, whose account of her family's coping with her own and her daughter's degenerative diseases she called *Celebration*. When my wife and I lost our second child, Grace, there was only one book that spoke deeply to both of us. This was *Lament for a Son*, in which the philosopher Nicholas Wolterstorff wrestles with the death of his and his wife Claire's son in a climbing accident.

Those public witnesses to the fact that it is possible for people to be overwhelmed by suffering and still emerge as 'compassionate, gentle human beings' are of immense importance. Wisdom gained this way is the costliest possible. The passion for wisdom – 'she is more precious than jewels, and nothing you desire can compare with her' (Proverbs 3:15) – applies here above all. The biblical wisdom tradition sounded its greatest depths in the book of Job's wrestling with suffering. Generation after generation in all traditions, the same wrestling has had to take place. Diamonds of wisdom-through-suffering have been produced under the most intense pressures, and if we find one it is to be treasured. It is very rarely that anything we suffer is without parallel in the experience of others. Those who go through their sufferings and produce (or even, in a sense, become) a diamond that can reflect the light of hope, are offering other people the most precious gift imaginable. So, in the face of the terrible blows that knock out of shape our lives and those of others, a basic resource is the wisdom that knows what it is like. If we treasure it we find that it multiplies: not only does it speak to us in our own sufferings but it can be passed on with extraordinary effects.

The continuation of Donald Nicholl's story about the survivor of Auschwitz illustrates this. That man slowly, over ten years, began to recover from his trauma, but this was accompanied by something terrible. His young wife

> descended by a parallel series of steps into a condition of terror comparable to the terror he had known in Auschwitz. That double terror is heartbreakingly described by her in a book which she later wrote, entitled *The Prisoner*. There we learn of the pathetic means by which she attempted to keep her terror at bay; that is, by reaching for food as her saviour. What happened to her in consequence was grotesque.
>
> As a result of eating so much and so frequently she grew incredibly fat, so fat indeed that taxi drivers used to refuse to allow her to ride in their taxis…
>
> The story could well, of course, have had a tragic ending. But … that was happily not the case. For by virtue of separating herself from her family and making a year-long pilgrimage she finally recovered.[3]

Nicholl gave *The Prisoner* to Arnold, another friend of his who had been in Auschwitz. It had an astonishing impact. The woman Arnold had been living with was suffering from the same 'Auschwitz fever', and as they read the book aloud to each other she began to be healed.

Nicholl's story is double-edged. It certainly shows the healing power of testimony by sufferers who have come through; but it also suggests why we often shy away not only from terrible suffering but even from those who have undergone it. We feel as if we too might be engulfed or 'infected'. To have these people in our heart is to find an abyss opening. Nicholl dares to go even further, and his words have implications for other communities which have been through appalling sufferings:

[At] the collective level the whole Jewish people has been a victim of the concentration camps and has caught 'Auschwitz fever'. Anyone who chooses to come close to the Jewish people, therefore, exposes himself to the risk of becoming infected, which is why so many high-minded people choose to distance themselves from Israel, pretending that the event of Auschwitz was nothing to do with them. I suspect, however, that their behaviour has less to do with high-mindedness than with a selfish fear of infection.[4]

This, as Nichol himself throughout his journal well recognizes, is dangerous ground. But it is also vital to the health of communities as much as individuals that in a world of great evil and suffering we all take responsibility for facing the truth, which comes to us most vividly in testimonies. How can a twentieth-century 'community of the heart' not include such witnesses and run such risks?

COMPASSION FOR OUR WEAKNESS

But testimony still seems at one remove from our own suffering. To know of people who plumbed the depths and came out more gentle and compassionate can just make us feel more miserable when we fail to live up to their example. Sometimes we are even ashamed of what it is that makes us suffer so much – an embarrassing habit or fear, a failure or humiliation that should be shrugged off, a physical ailment which is minor by comparison with others, a repeated sin, the shame and oppression of being in debt. Most of us have not faced torture or cancer or concentration camps, but we still suffer. The shape of our lives can be distorted by multiple pressures which may seem quite small to outsiders, yet cumulatively can lead to desperation. But whether our sufferings are less or more dramatic we long for more than the examples of other sufferers. We long for compassion.

When someone has compassion on us we find ourselves really seen, heard, attended to. In our suffering we involuntarily cry out (a wide range of our behaviour can count as 'crying out'). We have all done it since we were babies, and we still long to be attended to. Suffering intensifies our longing: can we find the 'mother' or 'father' we need? Will anyone have that quality of attention which springs from deep concern for us?

Compassionate attention is a complex matter, and there is no guarantee that, especially if we are suffering acutely, we will even recognize it. We easily regress to being like children who kick and scream and 'hate' their parents. But, granted all the complexities, this is something that most of us in most situations know whether we are receiving or not – and, indeed, the kicking and screaming may only be possible with people whose care for us we trust.

The agony is that, while we desperately need compassionate attention, we cannot guarantee it. It cannot be manipulated, bought, fabricated or produced to any formula. Someone has to offer it, freely and responsibly. Then they have to go on faithfully offering it. This makes us so vulnerable that we go to great lengths to find alternative forms of security. We deny or suppress our need. Or we become stoical, resigned to not having it met. Or we settle on more 'reliable' forms of comfort – drink, work, all sorts of addictions or escapes. Or we become aggressive against ourselves or others. Or we develop forms of relationship which attempt the impossible: compassionate attention without the vulnerability. The list could continue for pages – each of us can fill in how we try to compensate for lack of compassionate attention and how we try to avoid the risks of relying on it.

If someone's attention is genuinely compassionate it does not stop at attentiveness: he or she is willing to speak, act, and even suffer with us and for us. It is in such passivity, as we receive their compassion, that the most powerful dynamics of our own feeling and activity are shaped. Amazed gratitude for such compassion can be the inspiration of a lifetime. Bitterness at being denied it can be almost as powerful – suffering can contract as well as expand. Compassion is the overwhelming which meets our suffering with full realism and enables an expansive movement of love and generosity.

In experiencing acts of compassion we are touching what is really important in world history. Before God, compassion is what matters most. At our point of need we recognize this. It is accidental whether these acts become widely known. Most are done by ordinary people in unspectacular situations. The 'last judgement' is perhaps best pictured as showing and confirming God's judgement on this sort of history. Matthew chapter 25 gives a list of the sorts of events that will prove to have been most signif- icant: feeding the hungry, giving drink to the thirsty, welcoming strangers, clothing the naked, visiting prisoners and caring for the sick. The story graphically shows a glimpse of the 'alternative history' which is woven into our lives by those people who, at our point of deepest need, have paid us compassionate attention. It is also an invitation to take our bearings from those events and, in our public as well as our private lives, to play our role in the ongoing drama of compassion.

HEALING WITHOUT MAGIC

Etty Hillesum, the Dutch Jewish woman mentioned earlier, wrote diaries and letters which tell of her remarkable transformation as she went through persecution, hiding, life in a transit camp to Auschwitz, and eventual transport to her death. In a long poem, *Variations*, Micheal O'Siadhail includes three quotations from her in six lines:

Lean and mellow as that voice of Etty Hillesum
Ripening in whispers and rumours of a coming pogrom:
To the last moment life has beauty and meaning.
Her passion hums the reed. *You can no longer do*
But can only be and accept. Then, her adieu:
We must be ready to act as a balm for all wounds.[5]

Together those quotations suggest a response to suffering and evil which might be summed up as trust in healing without magic.

Life has beauty and meaning

Suffering and evil go deep in life and tempt us to despair of it being beautiful and meaningful. Because our suffering is so intolerable we are also tempted to try magical, quick-fix solutions which do not do justice to the depth of the problems. If there is to be healing it needs to be measured by the ability to sustain and even enhance appreciation of the glory of life while at the same time being utterly realistic about all that destroys life.

That quality of healing calls for Etty's perspective of 'the last moment'. Her diaries show her facing death open-eyed. In previous chapters I have discussed this phenomenon: fully vibrant living is possible only when the reality of death is not repressed – for example, in the L'Arche community which accompanied Antonio in his dying and allowed his beauty to appear.[6] Taking to heart testimonies such as those of Etty, Antonio, Sheila Cassidy or other members of the community of sufferers, opens up new dimensions of beauty and meaning, and even changes our criteria for judging them. But there is much more to the kaleidoscope of life's beauty and meaning, and the next chapter will go further into that.

The long apprenticeship of assent

There is another moment in suffering which is mysterious and yet is attested in many traditions and lives. This is the 'willed passivity' in which we 'no longer do/ But can only be and accept'. O'Siadhail elsewhere meditates on this in three of its classic biblical forms in the Book of Job, the 'suffering servant' of Isaiah chapter 53, and Jesus saying yes to the 'cup of suffering' in the Garden of Gethsemane just before his arrest:

A stumbling over stones of ancient agonies.
The self-same questions as once in Job's cry.

Even the same answers. How it's beyond us.
A threshold. *Hast thou with him spread out the sky?*

Departures. Successions. A zillionth in a hugeness.
My words are frivolous. How can I try to reply?

146

Or because you've loved, you're trusting to surprise.
One final show of confidence in Madam Jazz.

Sacrifice. The old song of the bruised servant.
Then, when the angel comes to want to say yes.

Stumbling over the stones of ancient agonies,
I begin this long apprenticeship of assent.'

Assent to suffering is a knife-edge. On one side are the wrong
sorts of passivity which give in to evil, fail to value life and health,
and glorify suffering as something good in itself. On the other
side are the wrong sorts of activity which make elimination of
suffering an absolute, strive above all for comfort and control, and
fail to see the superficiality and boredom of a world without risk
of things going wrong. In between is the apprenticeship which
can only be served with those who know the trade of suffering
and have learnt when, and how, to accept it and assent to it.

They recognize that great suffering is overwhelming and has
therefore simply to be undergone. There comes a point when the
questions change. Then we no longer ask about how to avoid a
particular suffering or even why it is happening to us. Instead, all
our resources are focused on how we might come through it, and
our ultimate question becomes (if we can learn from those who
know the trade best): what is it for? The basic trust is that
suffering, evil and even death do not have the last word about life.
So Gandhi, in Richard Attenborough's film about him, stays
facing the police at the salt mines, and one after another he and his
followers receive sickening club-blows to their heads and bodies.
So Jesus in Gethsemane accepts the cup and continues on the way
to his crucifixion.

Balm for all wounds

What healing can we hope for in our suffering? The longing is for something magical, the quick fix, the miraculous touch or medicine, the dramatic release. And occasionally the miracle does happen. One of the best-attested facts about Jesus is that he healed people. God is a God of surprises, hears prayer, and has compassion on suffering. It is always right to ask.

But it is clear too that prayer is not magic or a slot machine. God is not a God of quick fixes and easy, instantaneous solutions. Signs of hope are given, but God is above all concerned with love and long-term faithfulness, with healing hearts, minds and communities as well as bodies. How can that be done unless people and groups are wholeheartedly involved over time? Healing has to be as radical and complex as the wound and hurt. Any realistic assessment of what thorough, long-term healing means in a world like ours must talk about costly and risky processes. 'Clinical interventions' have their place, but they deal with a very limited range of problems. If deep suffering and evil could be dealt with by formulas, techniques and a problem-solving mentality, then our civilization above all should have been able to make progress in coping with war, poverty, debt, violence, addiction, family break-up, injustice, and the multitude of other evils and miseries which fill the media.

In his brief ministry Jesus did his best to give short-term help in healings and feedings. But the thrust of his teaching was to get at the roots of evil and suffering, and his message of the Kingdom of God was about a healing which involved love, trust, compassion, forgiveness, and radically inclusive hospitality. He faced the fact that that sort of healing can only be offered by those who embody it, whatever the cost. So he in his own life embodied it and paid the cost with his life. He gave his life in the mysterious exchange which was discussed in the last chapter. This is the 'healing exchange' at the heart of Christian faith and worship.

How does it heal? The Last Supper gives a clue. There Jesus identified the bread and wine with his body and blood. He invites followers into the sort of costly and risky process in which he was engaged on the night before he died. To eat the bread and drink the wine unites us with him on his way to crucifixion. The 'good news' is that his compassionate, vulnerable love is the way of healing – through death. The trust is that there is no depth of suffering, evil or death that cannot be plumbed by him. He and those who live and die like him are 'balm for all wounds'.

WOUNDS OF DEATH, CRIES OF GRIEF

Yet it is a very strange balm. If anything, bringing God into it seems to intensify suffering in the way described by von Hügel at the beginning of this chapter. I remember a close friend saying how much her faith in God seemed to have increased her anguish in comparison to the acceptance by her atheist husband that 'it is just part of the way things are'. Bereavement is perhaps the most universal form of suffering, because human mortality is 100 per cent. It is therefore one of the most profound shapers of human life. What is it to have our lives shaped by grief before God?

Nicholas Wolterstorff's *Lament for a Son* tries to answer this with agonizing honesty. He describes the terrible transformation of his life by the death of his son, Eric. The past was changed: the joy of good memories became a source of pain. He felt an impera-tive to remember, to resist amnesia, but this increased the agony. Everything became charged with the potential of being a reminder of Eric. There were also regrets, and the need for forgiveness. In the present, the zest for living vanished – that awful, wearying heaviness of grief. 'The worst days now are holidays: Thanksgiving, Christmas, Easter, Pentecost, birthdays, weddings, 31 January – days meant as festivals of happiness and joy now are days of tears. The gap is too great between day and heart.'[8] Looking to the future,

> it is the *neverness* that is so painful. *Never again* to be here with us – never to sit with us at table, never to travel with us, never to laugh with us, never to cry with us; never to embrace us as he leaves for school, never to see his brothers and sisters marry. All the rest of our lives we must live without him. Only our death can stop the pain of his death.[9]

So the whole of time, past, present and future, was transformed by grief. Wolterstorff laments – and as a philosopher and Christian his lament takes the form of crying out anguished, searching questions to God. If nothing else achieves it, suffering can make our faith interrogative.

Wolterstorff raises question after question, page after page:

Will the pain of the *no more* always outweigh the gratitude for the *once was*?

Why did he climb that mountain?

Is such shattering of love *beyond* meaning for us, the breaking of meaning – mystery, terrible mystery?

Can sadness be relieved, or can one only pass it by, very slowly?

Did something demonic take place there near the peak of the Ellmauerhalt? Or is this a specimen of mythical thinking that 'modern man' ought to eliminate from his mind?

Is there no music which *fits* our brokenness? How am I to sing in this desolate land, where there is always one too few?

What do I do with my God-forgiven regrets?

Will my eyes adjust to this darkness? In the dark, is it best to wait in silence?

Am I deluded in believing that in God the question shouted out by the wounds of the world has its answer? Am I deluded in believing that some day I will know the answer? Am I deluded in believing that once I know the answer, I will see that love has conquered?

Why don't you raise my son now? Why must your conquest of sin and death and suffering be so achingly slow?

Why do you permit yourself to suffer, O God? If the death of the devout costs you dear (Psalm 116:15), why do you permit it? Why do you not grasp joy? What does this mean for life, that God suffers? In what respects do we mirror God? Do we also mirror God in our suffering? Is it our glory to suffer?

Why 'Blessed are those who mourn'? Why does he hail the world's mourners? Who then are the mourners? Why isn't Love-*without*-suffering the meaning of things? Why is *suffering* -Love the meaning? Why does God endure his suffering? Why does he not at once relieve his agony by relieving ours?

This gaping wound in my chest – does it heal?

Is our suffering ever redemptive? Can suffering over death – not living at peace with death but *suffering* in the face of death – bring peace? That the radiance which emerges from acquaintance with grief is a blessing to others is familiar, though perplexing: how can we treasure the radiance while struggling against what brought it about? How can we thank God for suffering's yield while asking for its removal? How do I sustain my 'No' to my son's early death while accepting with gratitude the opportunity offered of becoming what otherwise I could never be? How do I receive my suffering as blessing while repulsing the obscene thought that God jiggled the mountain to make *me* better?

I wonder how it will all go when God raises him and the rest of us from the dead? Giving us new bodies seems no great problem, but how is he going to fit us all together into his city? Will I hear Eric say some day, *really* now I mean: 'Hey, Dad, I'm back'?[10]

Wrestling with all those questions, Wolterstorff gives far fewer answers, but the answers he does give distil a wisdom that can painfully expand faith, hope and love. 'I will not look away from Eric dead'[11] is the realism central to his response. He refuses the many escapes from death and grief. At the heart of that is his refusal to look away from Jesus Christ crucified. He follows through (for the first time in his life, he says) the line from the cross to the suffering, compassionate heart of God. He knows no firm answer to many of his questions, but he confesses: 'Through the prism of my tears I have seen a suffering God.'[12] He rethinks why it might be that we cannot see God's face and live: the sorrow in that face would be too much for us.

And great mystery: to redeem our brokenness and lovelessness the God who suffers with us did not strike some mighty blow of power but sent his beloved son to suffer *like* us, through his suffering to redeem us from suffering and evil.

Instead of explaining our suffering God shares it.[13]

To be in the image of this God is to mourn:

Who then are the mourners? The mourners are those who have caught a glimpse of God's new day, who ache with all their being for that day's coming, and who break out in tears when confronted with its absence. They are the ones who realize that in God's realm of peace there is no one blind, and who ache whenever they see someone unseeing. They are the ones who realize that in God's realm there is no one hungry, and who ache whenever they see someone starving. They are the ones who realize that in God's realm there is no one falsely accused, and who ache whenever they see someone imprisoned unjustly. They are the ones who realize that in God's realm there is no one who fails to see God, and who ache whenever they see someone unbelieving. They are the ones who realize that in God's realm there is no one who suffers oppression, and who ache whenever they see someone beat down. They are the ones who realize that in God's realm there is no one without dignity, and who ache whenever they see someone treated with indignity. They are the ones who realize that in God's realm of peace there is neither death nor tears, and who ache whenever they see someone crying tears over death. The mourners are aching visionaries...

The Stoics of antiquity said: Be calm. Disengage yourself. Neither laugh nor weep. Jesus says: Be open to the wounds of the world. Mourn humanity's mourning, weep over humanity's wounds, be in agony over humanity's agony. But do so in the good cheer that a day of peace is coming.[14]

That is the expansive side of grief. It can enlarge our sympathy, our compassion, and our capacity for joy as well as for suffering. It increases our aching for the new day, and knows that the true balm for this wound requires that the wound stay open:

I shall try to keep the wound from healing, in recognition of our living still in the old order of things. I shall try to keep it from healing, in solidarity with those who sit beside me on humanity's mourning bench.[15]

THE OVERWHELMING OF DEATH

When Sheila Cassidy was writing *Good Friday People* she stayed at the Irish monastery of Glenstal, and there had her understanding of Easter revolutionized by an icon of Christ's descent into hell. Christ was trampling and destroying hell's instruments of torture:

Suddenly I saw not Adam and the Fathers of the Church being rescued from hell, but my own people. If the risen Christ was trampling down the bronze gates and freeing the trapped souls in Hades, then surely he must have been there in exactly the same way for Ita and her friends trapped in that hideous death van on the Salvadorean hillside. I had always known that Christ was there, suffering with them, but I had never thought of him as risen, as Christ the valiant in war rescuing his people.

I found the idea enormously exciting and somehow infinitely more logical than a quiet and dignified transition from death to new life. Suddenly I saw resurrection as a magnificent explosion into joy and life and laughter, just as Lazarus leapt eagle-like from the tomb.[16]

She links hell with the prison of the depressed, the tortured, the starving. It is not a matter of taking the imagery literally – rather, the imagery is not nearly literal enough: language is unable to do justice either to the terrors that people go through or to the overwhelming liberation and joy that God offers through and beyond death.

What is traditionally called 'the harrowing of hell' is an attempt to explore the significance of that fascinating day, Holy Saturday, the day of silence between Good Friday and Easter Sunday. It is perhaps no accident that people should be drawn to it in a century such as ours. Others (including some who do not confess Christian faith, such as George Steiner) have also been gripped anew by this day as they have wrestled with the evil, suffering, and what Edith Wyschogrod calls the 'man-made mass death' of our times.

Sheila Cassidy moves through the Orthodox liturgy for Holy Saturday. At its heart is the meeting of two great overwhelmings, darkness and light. 'Deep in the darkest moment of the passion the light forces its way under the door. True, it is Good Friday but it is also Great and Holy Saturday, Christ is dying but he is also rising.'[17] It is an unimaginable moment, and the New Testament is utterly silent about it. Canticle One in the liturgy stretches to express it:

O Lord my God, I will sing to Thee a funeral hymn, a song at Thy burial: for by Thy burial Thou hast opened for me the gates of life, and by Thy death Thou hast slain death and hell.

All things above and all beneath the earth quaked with fear at Thy death, as they beheld Thee, O my Saviour, upon Thy throne on high and in the tomb below. For beyond our understanding Thou dost lie before our eyes, a corpse yet the very source of life.[18]

To refuse, with Wolterstorff and Cassidy, to look away either from the suffering of humanity or from the crucified Jesus, leads us with them through Holy Saturday. That day is about 'trampling down death by death'. It is the inconceivable good news of someone crying out (as Christ does in that liturgy) to the dead dead and to us, the living dead: Awake! Have light! Come forth! You were made for life and love: meet your Bridegroom!

ARMS AROUND OUR SORROW

So our suffering can be 'held' as we participate in a drama of cosmic scope, whose characters figure in scriptures and liturgies. It can further be held through the men and women who witness to the capacity to come through great suffering as 'compassionate, gentle human beings'. They allow us to glimpse the ways our lives might be reshaped for good because of suffering. We would never choose the blows and wrenchings that seem only to contort and distort our lives. Yet, when they happen, we have great need of instruction from those who have been these ways before us.

But our most intense need and desire is for the drama and the instruction to be incarnate right beside us in someone who is compassionate and gentle with us. When suffering assaults us, who is there to hold us? Micheal O'Siadhail's poem 'Loss' evokes the ordinary suffering of grief, and also the possibility of finding (and offering) something beyond healing:

The last summer he walked slower, chose to linger.
Pausing in a laneway, he ran a thumb along the seam
of an old garden wall – 'Those joints need pointing,'
he warned; attentive, we saw in his face some strange
play of inward movement. On request we drove to Meath;
those fields a dozen times the size of his own

pleasured his eye. At Christmas leaning on the window sill,
lovingly, he gazed over a few loamy acres towards Gola.
In mid-January, cutting back briars, he fell with his scythe.

Several years later, I waken deep into the night,
hear you sobbing to yourself. It's Patrick's Eve,
that evening your father used to return after
his winter exile, a labourer in Scotland; three
eager children watch the dark beyond Dunlewy.
Now, at last, the bus's headlamps arc the sky –
overjoyed you race the lights to meet him at Bunbeg.
Tonight, here by your side I listen, then kissing
your forehead, throw my arms around your sorrow.[19]

SEVEN

KALEIDOSCOPE – RESURRECTION, JOY AND FEASTING

Joy may be a greater scandal than evil, suffering or death. Some people have a realism that can come to terms with the darker side but cannot cope with something that seems too good to be true. Crucifixion was a fairly routine matter in the Roman Empire at the time of Jesus, but resurrection was not.

For the first Christians the resurrection of the crucified Jesus was an overwhelming event that filled their lives and their horizons. If Christ was truly risen then everything was different. They stretched language to try to express it: it meant new birth, new creation, new hope, acceptance by God, a fresh start in forgiveness, new community across old barriers, an inundation of the Holy Spirit, and the presence of the risen Jesus Christ. The dominant note in all this was joy. This chapter explores the shape of living whose tone is set by resurrection joy.

THE TEST OF JOY

Joys as well as sufferings test us. How do we cope with a honeymoon, the safe arrival of a child, a new friendship? It is common for the best things to cause considerable anxiety. How can we do justice to them? What will they reveal about us? Will we be able to contain them?

The answer to the last question should be: No! There is something explosive, excessive and overflowing about joy which resists containment. There can even be a wildness, a sense that life is not domesticated and predictable, and that can be very threatening, as our usual boundaries and sense of identity are challenged to open up to something new and beyond our previous experience. Back in chapter 1 we looked at falling in love as described by O'Siadhail's poem 'Out of the Blue', with its notes of adventure, amazement, 'subtle jazz of the new familiar', and love shifting the boundaries of our being. We have come at this theme of overwhelming from many directions in the chapters since then, but now we are trying to appreciate the most radical of all.

Joy tests us by inviting us to be transformed by it. Most of us are deeply distrustful of the possibility of joy. There are good reasons for our distrust: the yearning for joy opens us to repeated disappointments, and the world is full of deceitful or over-hyped promises of joy. To be transformed by joy means trust, even surrender, and that is a massive risk. There is no avoiding risk, and once the process of transformation begins we cannot tell where it will lead – what will happen to me in marriage to this woman, or as the parent of this child? Nevertheless, we make judgements about risks, and invitations of joy are not accepted without examination. The same double testing is called for in relation to resurrection joy. We need to face it as a joy that can transform our whole life, testing us by giving us something, someone, uncontainable. We also need to test it by examining it to see whether it should be trusted and surrendered to. We will deal with the latter first.

Examining the invitation to joy

The resurrection of Jesus Christ is God's way of inviting us into joy. Jesus himself gave a message of God's unimaginable generosity, inviting everyone into the feast of the Kingdom of God. 'Enter into your master's joy' is the ultimate welcome. He was also clear-eyed about all that prevents or spoils joy – sin, evil, suffering, death, and the disbelief which rejects an invitation that seems too good to be true. Facing all those showed the realism of the joy he promised. It is itself a tested joy, to the point of crucifixion. The double overwhelming of suffering and joy is embodied in one person, and the heart of the good news is that Jesus Christ is our joy. He can be rejoiced in without reservation.

But can this news be trusted? Can we surrender to him with confidence? This is partly a question of truth. Here we need to be very careful. It is easy to think of testing for truth as a matter of having agreed measurements which we then apply to particular cases. But what measurements do we apply to God? If anything is clear from the New Testament witnesses it is that the resurrection is a God-sized event. It did not fit their expectations and categories – the disciples 'disbelieved for joy, and wondered' (Luke 24:41), 'when they saw him they worshipped him, but some doubted' (Matthew 28:17). There is no ready-made worldview into which it fits. As a God-sized event, the same considerations apply to it as to the reality of God: if we think we have a framework that contains it, then we have not grasped the sort of event it is.

As a scholar and theologian, for years I have studied the resurrection and writings about it. My conclusions are in essence very simple, though to back them up adequately would take many books.

First and foremost, it is a matter of what sort of God (if any) is believed in. I believe in the God who created the universe and who cannot therefore be known like an object within the universe. There is no standpoint from which God can be inspected. This God is free in relation to creation, and is free to be God in ways which are new to us. Raising Jesus Christ from the dead fits with a creator God who is free to surprise us. So my framework is one in which this God is God. It is tested every day of my life, intellectually and practically, and I have a very limited understanding of it, but I do not believe there is any bigger or more fundamental framework by which to judge it.

Other people approach the resurrection with very different frameworks. Often they do not admit them openly but claim to be looking 'objectively' or 'from the outside'. They inevitably do have frameworks and criteria, however, and the only way there can be fruitful debate is if these too are debated. The resurrection is an event 'than which none greater can be conceived' (to use Anselm's phrase about God), so it challenges our very idea of reality. We can try to assess it without taking the creator God into account, but in that case we need to be clear about what we are doing: we are opting for some other account of reality; and we are not talking about what the New Testament is witnessing to.

Second, there is no avoiding trusting (or distrusting) testimony to the resurrection. Whatever it was, it took place at a particular time and place. As with any historical event, there is no way we can re-run history in order to check what happened. Testimony is the only way we have access to the past which we cannot ourselves remember. So we are always, like a jury in a trial, faced with decisions about whether or not to trust the witnesses. It is not too much to say that the Church is the community of those who trust the testimony of the first witnesses to the resurrection.

Since then there have been two millennia of cross-examination and speculation. My verdict on what I have studied is that the original witnesses have by no means been proved untrustworthy, and that it is reasonable to believe their main message: that the crucified Jesus Christ is risen. There are still huge questions, and many ways of interpreting their testimony, but the fundamental issue is their basic reliability, on which they themselves were willing to stake their lives.

Third, this truth is inevitably self-involving. It cannot be adequately taken in unless we begin to be transformed. It is not just our ideas about reality that are challenged: our commitments, hopes, desires and behaviour are involved too. This is because it is not just 'an event': it is about the new presence of a particular person, and we can never relate adequately to people unless we are willing to be affected by them. Part of the authenticity of the first witnesses lies in the way they were transformed and lived the rest of their lives. So the truth of the resurrection is not a truth about which we can appropriately say 'How interesting!' and then go on to some other investigation. It has the urgency of the most relevant news – like someone shouting 'Fire!' or whispering 'Will you marry me?' This leads us on from the trustworthiness of the joyful news to its testing of the shape of our living.

Expanded by joy

Even as we begin to test the resurrection we find that it is also testing us – our notions of God, of what is possible, of whom we trust. The further we go with it the more radically we are tested. Is it really the case that God wants to share God's own joy with us? If so, what will it mean for us?

162

God does not coerce into joy, but there is always more on offer than we can take. There are as many ways into Christian joy as there are people, and the variety of testimonies is endless. Some begin in a burst of joy; others are far more hesitant, and only very slowly wake up to the intense joy at the core of faith. There are also different qualities of joy through life, culminating in the matured peacefulness of those who have been through great suffering, and have had their capacity for joy expanded and deepened in the process. But whatever our experience, if the background for the ups and downs of our lives includes the Psalms, the hymns of many Christian traditions and the New Testament, then we can never forget that joy is the accompanying and ultimate note of faith in the God of creation and resurrection. We are created for joy, and salvation is inseparable from it. The First Letter of Peter sums it up powerfully, writing to Christians entering the period beyond the death of the first witnesses to the resurrection:

> Blessed be the God and Father of our Lord Jesus Christ! By his great mercy we have been born anew to a living hope through the resurrection of Jesus Christ from the dead ... Without having seen him you love him; although you do not now see him you believe in him and rejoice with an indescribable and glorious joy, for you are receiving the outcome of your faith, the salvation of your souls. (1 Peter 1:3, 8–9)

We are therefore constantly stretched to accommodate more joy, and this affects not only the tone of our lives but its very shape. Celebration and praise of the God of joy become a *cantus firmus*, with accompanying counterpoints of rejoicing in other people, rejoicing in truth and goodness, rejoicing in creation, and in all sorts of creativity, play and work. It is a constant, gentle, and sometimes vigorous testing, inviting us to be more appreciatively open to God, people and the world, expanding our capacity to cope with the infinite joy that God desires to share with us.

FEASTING

Let us savour a good meal for a while, in Micheal O'Siadhail's 'Delight':

Let the meal be simple. A big plate
of mussels, warm bread with garlic,
and enough mulled wine to celebrate.

Being here. I open a hinged mussel
pincering a balloon of plump meat
from the blue angel wings of a shell.

A table's rising decibels of fun.
Such gossip. A story caps a story.
Banter. Then, another pun on a pun.

Iced yoghurt snipes at my temples.
My tongue matches a strawberry's heart
with its rough skin of goose-pimples.

Conversations fragment. Tête-à-tête,
a confidence passes between two guests.
A munch of oatcake thickens my palate.

Juicy fumes of a mango on my breath.
(A poem with no end but delight.)
I knife to the oblong host of its pith.

Wine sinks its ease to the nerve-ends.
Here are my roots. I feast on faces.
Boundless laughter. A radiance of friends.[1]

There is something ultimate about a feast like that. It is beyond physical or social necessity, and, like the people who celebrate it, it is an end in itself. But an open end, with 'no end but delight'! The 'boundless laughter' reminds me of the poet Patrick Kavanagh's description of the resurrection as 'a laugh freed/for ever and ever'. Like the resurrection, feasts have the intensity and expansiveness of good laughter, transforming life and whetting the appetite for more.

I like the vision of the Church which sees it as a succession of feasts. It is rooted in Israel's festivals, above all the Passover celebrating release from slavery in Egypt. It also remembers Jesus the party-goer, with his parables of the Kingdom of God as a feast, and his practice and teaching of hospitality towards the poor and marginalized – those who are not able to invite us back. Then there was the Last Supper and his urging, while sharing bread and wine, to 'do this in remembrance of me', initiating centuries of variations on that meal all over the world. And all through that history there have been greater and lesser festivals year by year.

So it is a community constituted by sharing meals. In this it is simply being human – what is more common to human communities? The vision of the feast of the Kingdom of God, when people come to sit down from north, south, east and west, is of a joy that no present community can contain. If each person is created in the image of the God of joy, we will never come to the end of enjoying each other's company and finding fresh occasions of joy.

This vision of promised joy has the most radical consequences now. No community can rest in its present level of hospitality towards others. All our actions towards others can be tested by whether they are in harmony with wholehearted feasting together eventually. What changes will have to happen in ourselves, our families and communities in order to be able fully to enjoy the company of other classes, races, religions, commitments, personality types and cultures? A fundamental point about the resurrection of Jesus is that it means this joy can begin to be experienced now: Jesus offers a hospitality which crosses all those barriers and leads us to shift our boundaries. It is worth meditating on the implications of this.

Any family which has had a baby born into it knows the joy of this but also the upheaval – not least at mealtimes. All schedules and priorities have to be reorganized in order to accommodate this joy. Now magnify it on a global scale to imagine the upheaval in our nations, religions and other communities that genuine feasting together 'as one family' would involve. Our identities, boundaries, habits and favourite menus would all be open to surprising transformations. The resurrected Jesus invites us to savour this in advance, and to create now in the present signs that this is the true reality. It is a promise of joys unlimited and transformations unimagined.

I suppose we all have our treasured examples of giving or receiving hospitality which has savoured of God's own feast. I think of just a few of my kaleidoscope of joys.

As a painfully shy first-year university freshman, an older student, Leslie Webb, week after week invited me into his rooms for coffee and toast. There, very slowly, in company with people who seemed to live in a world of culture and intellect beyond anything I could take part in, I thawed and found my tongue. Not only that, I was introduced there to Micheal O'Siadhail for the first time.

In Turkey, travelling with a friend and very little money for two months, high on the Anatolian plateau, after a dusty journey in a lorry, a householder in a village insisted we join him for dinner. I had never eaten eggs before, but they made up most of the meal. So it was impossible to refuse them, and I have enjoyed them ever since.

In America two Jewish New Yorkers became my closest friends, which meant that my first immersion in that amazing country was punctuated by a succession of family meals, take-aways, ice creams, and Passover: a whole new world.

In inner-city Birmingham I think of an interweaving succession of larger church meals, when a varied congregation would get together, and of smaller meals in our home group. Often a key ingredient was Caribbean cookery – chicken, meats, sweet potato, mango, cakes. It was here that the theme of the face of Christ gripped me first: 'I feast on faces.' When I had just become engaged to my wife, an elderly West Indian, Iris Wright, who had had a very tough life and now had failing health, invited us round for 'tea', which turned out to be a full-scale four-course celebratory meal.

The list could go on: Christmas Day celebrated with two Thai Buddhists; a very long evening, turning into morning, with two other couples when each of the six of us shared our life stories; the messy, joyful meals at L'Arche; silent meals on retreat which bonded better than speech; reunion meals with old friends; and the succession of family celebrations, Cambridge college feasts, conference meals, and Eucharists that have overflowed into breakfasts or lunches.

Many of those meals have been shot through with sorrow, difficulties of many sorts, and great seriousness: joy is by no means to be equated with uninterrupted happiness or painlessness. On the contrary, the depth and intensity of the joy and the seriousness can go together. It is a common observation that often those communities with most experience of suffering know best how to celebrate.

FEASTS OF BEAUTY AND TRUTH

Hospitality is a complex matter. There are decisions about guests, menu, time and place, the work of providing and preparing a room and food and drink, and the actual performance of hosting or being entertained, with perhaps music, dancing, games or other entertainment as well as conversation. It amounts to an extraordinary co-ordination and interweaving of elements, and any one of them going wrong can affect the joy. To have a vision of the feast of the Kingdom of God, and to want to have foretastes of it now, is therefore to be concerned for many things and people coming together. Perhaps the biggest vision of all is given in one verse of the Letter to the Ephesians which speaks of God having

a plan for the fullness of time, to gather up [unify, recapitulate, consummate] all things in Christ, things in heaven and things on earth. (Ephesians 1:10)

That is a stupendous picture of Jesus Christ as the host of the universe, entertaining everything and everyone. Let us stretch our imaginations to begin to conceive the significance of that. It of course embraces the literal hospitality we have been discussing, with feasting as the practice that can most clearly hint at the ultimate destiny to which God is inviting us. That in turn involves healing of relationships, forgiveness of wrongs, justice, and all that makes for the sort of peace in which people can enjoy each other across their differences.

The arts

But it stretches our imaginations yet further. Think of the forms of gathering and uniting that go on in the arts. One of Ephesians' own favourite images is of a building – architecture is in some ways the supreme art, uniting so many trades, skills and materials in the shaping of habitable space. Poetry and other literature make new gatherings of words and meanings, painting brings together colours and forms, music configures sounds, drama presents the shape of life itself in plots and characters, and so on. This, at its best, is a feast of meaning and beauty, generating powerful forms of communication that help to join people together in cultures.

Micheal O'Siadhail's poem 'Courtesy' explores this image of the great artists, composers and writers as the shapers of our lives in 'ecstasies I'll never understand'. They inspire a continuing sharing of courteous hospitality and the formation of his own 'genes' as a poet:

I bring my basketful to serve
Our table. Everything mine is yours.
Everything. Without reserve.

169

Poems to which I still revert.
Gauguin. Matisse. Renoir's pear-shaped women.
Music I've heard. Blessed Schubert.

Ecstasies I'll never understand –
Mandelstam's instants of splendour, the world
A plain apple in his hand.

Lost faces. Those whose heirs
I was. My print-out of their genes,
Seed and breed of forebears.

Whatever I've become – courtesy
Of lovers, friends or friends of friends.
All those traces in me.

The living and dead. My sum
Of being. A host open and woundable.
Here I am![2]

That 'sum of being', recapitulating the traces of the past, and offered to others 'without reserve' by a woundable host, makes a superb interpretation of Ephesians 1:10. O'Siadhail himself is fascinated by jazz as a realization of this. It is as if the roots of jazz in the African-American slave experience of suffering endurance, mingled with an extraordinary capacity for hope and celebration, makes it ideal for drawing us into a joy that has already faced the worst in life. Here is O'Siadhail's celebration of the great jazz trumpeter Louis Armstrong ('Satchmo'):

Always this urge to begin and rebegin.
Armstrong's trumpet swings and skips
O when the saints go marching in.

As if rhythms keep needing to recompose
This determined joy of passionate blues,
His melody shatters the stricter tempos.

He can't imagine it and still he must,
A garden where beginnings and ends collide.
Every image is trying to widen our trust.

Valhalla's vivid and endless carouse.
Blacks downing burdens by the riverside.
Promise of a father's many-mansioned house.

For me just my friends. O my jazz eternal
Give me their warmth, the talk, the glory
In the faces of saints, boisterous and carnal.

O I want to be in that number when...
His trumpet ransacking the melody's secret.
Satchmo of the horn, march on, march on.[3]

The improvisations 'widen our trust' as they swing, skip, and risk reimagining heaven where the saints march in with 'determined joy' and the atmosphere is the opposite of boring. Perhaps one of our greatest blockages is our inability to imagine full joy – glory in faces, 'boisterous and carnal'. The scandal of this joy is a revolutionary and subversive response to slavery, oppression and death.

The sciences, scholarship and the life of the mind

What it might mean to unify all things also includes the many branches of knowledge. Think of the patient searching out of truth that goes on in each of the natural sciences, the human sciences, the scholarly and literary disciplines: endlessly making connections and distinctions, developing hypotheses and theories, trying to understand reality better. Then think of all the more practical aspects which involve implications for changing the world of nature or society or meaning. There is another feast of many courses here, and at the heart of it are joys of wonder, discovery, insight, and making things work.

Dietrich Bonhoeffer had an astonishing burst of intellectual creativity during his years in prison before his execution in 1945. His letters and papers show him reading widely when he was allowed books – in history, poetry, novels, early Christian life and thought, theology, science, philosophy, and much else. His thinking took leaps and made new connections. There was a concentrated energy and discipline combined with adventurous freedom. The word he used about those thinkers he learnt most from was the Latin *hilaritas*. It conveys a cheerful confidence, a joy in the sheer goodness of seeking and finding truth and wisdom. Without it the feast is dull.

My own first taste of real theology was when I accidentally came upon Bonhoeffer's *Ethics* as a teenager. Despite being out of my depth I was gripped by the integrated intensity of thought, faith and practicality, and recognized that I had tasted something new in the 'life of the mind'.

Years later, when studying classics, I remember being grasped for hours by this passage from Plato's Seventh Letter:

If the hearer has the divine spark which makes the love of wisdom congenial to him and fits him for its pursuit, the way

described to him [Plato has just described its rigours] appears so
wonderful that he must follow it with all his might if life is to be
worth living ... Only after long partnership in a common life
devoted to this very thing does truth flash upon the soul, like a
flame kindled by a leaping spark, and once it is born there it
nourishes itself thereafter.[4]

It was another taste of the ecstasy of intellectual awakening, and a
glimpse of the 'common life' that allows it to happen.

That thrill has been repeated many times in different ways – the
book that cannot be put down; the conversation that takes off and
soars from one fresh insight to the next; the seminar that cumulatively, week after week, develops a subject and draws the unsus-
pected best out of the participants; the research student's work
that achieves breakthrough; the process of writing that leads my
thought somewhere it has not been before; the sobering (even
humiliating), yet somehow liberating, demolition of a shaky
hypothesis for good reasons; the slow development of a position
on a major topic in conversation with living and dead thinkers
over many years.

We say that we 'entertain' ideas. Our mind is shaped through
the intellectual hospitality of recognizing and welcoming
meaning, truth and wisdom. The most intelligent and understanding people from the past, and from all round the world
today, can be our hosts and serve us the dishes they do best. We
taste the joy of hospitality across time and space as an ancient
Greek and a modern Lithuanian philosopher, a Hebrew and a
Hindu wisdom writer, an Irish poet, a Muslim social anthropolo-
gist, a German novelist and a black womanist come into conversation with each other. Above all there are our own teachers,
who have spread their feast before us, advised us about which

invitations to accept, and encouraged us to try our own recipes. We discover the delicate interplay between being host and being guest. We begin to cook for others, to try out new dishes, to bring together guests who have never met before.

Then, occasionally, there is something further, as hospitality becomes friendship. It could happen a great deal more frequently if we had the time and energy; but the richness, complexity and concentration of full friendship means that our core 'community of the heart' has to be quite small. But, when it is possible, there must be few joys greater than this union of heart and mind which, year after year, pursues the search for understanding in trust and love.

THE HOSPITALITY OF GOD

Perichoresis is a Greek term from dancing, describing the circling and interweaving of a dance. It was daringly taken up by the early Church to suggest what goes on in the very life of God. It is worthwhile trying to understand why.

The resurrection of the crucified Jesus was an explosive event which transformed the bereaved disciples into a joyful community. As a God-sized event it was inexhaustibly rich, and its implications included a development in how God was identified. The God of Abraham, Isaac, Jacob and Moses, who was free to identify himself in new ways at different periods, was now seen as the God who raised Jesus Christ from the dead and poured out the Holy Spirit. This drama of crucifixion, resurrection and Pentecost was now at the heart of how God was known and worshipped. In the New Testament we see the implications beginning to be drawn, as Jesus Christ and the Holy Spirit are embraced in references to God. Paul and John go furthest in this, and generate a dynamic of intensive discussion in later generations.

Central to this discussion was the conviction that, to be true to the crucifixion, resurrection and Pentecost, it was vital to identify God in terms of Father, Son and Holy Spirit in their interrelationship. Worship showed this best, and the Church found itself using the language of the Trinity in worship before it worked out its controversial grammar.

But 'grammar' is not a very exciting image. At the heart of this vision of God is a vision of love. God creates out of love and always transcends creation. God also is utterly committed in love to creation and to its history, to the point of self-involvement in the human person of Jesus Christ. And God is a self-distributing God, continually overflowing in love through the Holy Spirit. To *be* love like this, God cannot be without internal relationship. So the least misleading way of talking of God as love is in terms of utter mutuality in dynamic life. This is where dancing gives a vivid image. It is communication in movement, with exchanges of role and place yet also differences and complementarity.

The hospitality of God therefore draws us into a life that at its core is like a dance of lovers. 'Weaving', the first part of Micheal O'Siadhail's poem 'Dance', describes this moment beyond the eating and drinking of the feast:

So tables aside! Any dance at all.
I'd loved our flight from the formal.
Our broken observance. Rock and Roll.
The Twist. Disco. Sweet and manic,
Our blare of rapture. Alone. Freelance.
But I yearn again for ritual, organic
Patterns, circlings, the whorled dance.

Sweated repetitiveness of reels that grew
To their ecstasy. A shrug. Yelped *yeoo*.
Quadrilles without the high buckled shoe,
Ribboned wigs, swallow-tailed elegance
Of Napoleon's court or Paris ballroom,
Figures needling an embroidery of dance,
Chaine-de-dames. Fan and perfume.

More a passionate sameness than grace.
Hospitality. Feelings of inclusiveness
As we lined up there. Face to face.
Expectant. Keats's lovers in the gaze
Of a moment but ready to step it out
Across the swollen belly of a vase.
Tableaux of memory wake in that shout:

Take the floor! The first battoned tone
Of a *céilí* band. *The Mason's Apron,*
Humours of Bandon. The Bridge of Athlone.
A swing. A turn. The skipping march.
Limerick's Walls, The Siege of Ennis.
Side-step and stoop under the arch.
Our linked arms. A scent of dizziness.

Openness. Again and again to realign.
Another face and the moves must begin
Anew. And we unfold into our design.
I want to dance for ever. A veil
Shakes between now-ness and infinity.
Touch of hands. Communal and frail.
Our courtesies weave a fragile city.[5]

That 'scent of dizziness' in our relationship with God is at the climax of one of the greatest poems of all, Dante's *Divine Comedy*. It is a story of multiple overwhelmings as the poet moves through Hell, Purgatory and Heaven. But why is this poem usually better known for its *Inferno* and its *Purgatorio* than for its *Paradiso*? We face again the scandal of joy. I do not think anyone has better evoked the dynamic perfection of heaven, overflowing with life, beauty and the delight of love. Dante, encouraged by the smiles and guidance of his great love, Beatrice, has his capacity for joy expanded as he passes through circle after circle of heaven.

Then in the final canto comes the vision of God.

> And I, who now was nearing Him who is
> the end of all desires, as I ought,
> lifted my longing to its ardent limit…
>
> From that point on, what I could see was greater
> than speech can show: at such a sight it fails –
> and memory fails when faced with such excess.[6]

Dante glimpsed the coherence of the whole universe:

> In its profundity I saw – ingathered
> and bound by love into one single volume –
> what, in the universe, seems separate, scattered.[7]

Then, as his 'sight grew stronger', the Trinity appeared as three rainbow-like circles in a *perichoresis* of light and colour. Finally, the ultimate overwhelming comes in a flash: it is a vision of the face of Jesus Christ, the human face of God at the heart of the

Trinity. And this unites his desire and will with

the Love that moves the sun and the other stars.[8]

That is the peaceful, uniform, cosmic dance of the heavenly bodies that crowned the medieval idea of God and the universe. But now reach back to the origins of Dante's vivid language. It takes us through centuries of envisioning God, back to the Book of Revelation:

At once I was in the Spirit, and lo, a throne stood in heaven, with one seated on the throne! And he who sat there appeared like jasper and carnelian, and round the throne was a rainbow that looked like an emerald ... From the throne issue flashes of lightning, and voices and peals of thunder... (Revelation 4:2–3, 5)

But we need to reach even further back to find the roots of this more turbulent vision. In the great vision of God at the opening of the Book of Ezekiel we find the imagery of storm, thunder, lightning, earthquake, rainbow, and, at the heart of it all, the human form. There is the wildness and unpredictability of some modern dance –

And the living creatures darted to and fro, like a flash of lightning. (Ezekiel 1:14)

But there is also the regularity of circles and wheels –

Now as I looked at the living creatures, I saw a wheel upon the earth beside the living creatures, one for each of the four of them ... their construction being as it were a wheel within the wheel

...And when the living creatures went, the wheels went beside them; and when the living creatures rose from the earth, the wheels rose. (Ezekiel 1:15–16, 19)

Ezekiel somehow holds together the darting and leaping with peaceful movement. Can we allow our vision of God to include other wilder and more surprising dance rhythms while even intensifying the exhilaration of love, joy and peace? The fourth and final part of O'Siadhail's 'Dance' sequence is called 'High':

Rhythm of now. Now the beat.
Forever. Forever.
Our *qui vive* of listening feet.
Sweetest seizure.

Such ecstasies as maddened Corybants:
A *bodhrán*'s crescendo,
Frenzy of bones knuckling the dance,
High wire of let-go.

A reel with all its plans. Drumbeat,
Steps or turns,
Stubborn ritual. Some dizzy heat
Of spirit yearns.

Forever. Forever. How to remember
In each move and pose,
Even the music's pitch and timbre
Crave repose?

Leaps in an infinite womb. I yield.
The dance's yes
Teeters on the rim of Achilles' shield.
Vertigo of gladness.'

How is that for a shape of living?

NOTES

Chapter 1

1 Micheal O'Siadhail, *Hail! Madam Jazz*, Newcastle-upon-Tyne, Bloodaxe, 1992, p. 84.
2 Ibid., p. 86.
3 Ibid., p. 118.
4 Micheal O'Siadhail, *A Fragile City*, Newcastle-upon-Tyne, Bloodaxe, 1995, p. 26.
5 *Hail! Madam Jazz*, p. 118.
6 Ibid.

Chapter 2

1 Micheal O'Siadhail, *Hail! Madam Jazz*, Newcastle-upon-Tyne, Bloodaxe, 1992, p. 118.
2 Nicholas Peter Harvey, *The Morals of Jesus*, London, Darton, Longman & Todd, 1991.
3 Ibid., pp. 94–5.
4 *Hail! Madam Jazz*, pp. 77–8.

Chapter 3

1 Dietrich Bonhoeffer, *Letters and Papers from Prison*, Enlarged Edition, London, SCM, 1971, p. 392.
2 Micheal O'Siadhail, *Hail! Madam Jazz*, Newcastle-upon-Tyne, Bloodaxe, 1992, p. 67.
3 Gordon Jackson, 'Homage to Max' in *The Quimper Poems*, Lincoln, Asgill Press, 1994, p. 30.
4 *Letters and Papers from Prison*, Enlarged Edition, p. 5.
5 Ibid., p. 7.
6 Ibid., pp. 8–9.
7 Ibid., pp. 3–17.
8 Donald Nicholl, *Holiness*, London, Darton, Longman & Todd, 1987, pp. 54–5.
9 Ibid., p. 163.

Chapter 4

1 Micheal O'Siadhail, *A Fragile City*, Newcastle-upon-Tyne, Bloodaxe, 1995, p. 21.
2 Micheal O'Siadhail, *Our Double Time*, due to be published 1998.
3 Micheal O'Siadhail, from 'Neighbour', *A Fragile City*, p. 40.
4 Micheal O'Siadhail, 'Francis to Clare' in *Hail! Madam Jazz*, Newcastle-upon-Tyne, Bloodaxe, 1992, p. 64.
5 Thomas Mann, *Joseph and His Brothers*, London, Penguin, 1978, p. 1181.
6 Dietrich Bonhoeffer, *The Cost of Discipleship*, London, SCM, 1964, p. 146.
7 Simon Barrington-Ward, *The Jesus Prayer*, Oxford, The Bible Reading Fellowship, 1996, pp. 19, 72.

8 *Letters from Baron Friedrich von Hügel to a Niece*, ed. with Introduction by Gwendolen Greene, London, J.M. Dent, 1928, pp. ix–x.

9 Ida Görres, *The Hidden Face. A Study of St Thérèse of Lisieux*, London, Burns and Oates, 1959, p. 308.

10 *Story of a Soul. The Autobiography of St Thérèse of Lisieux*, Washington DC, ICS Publications, 1976, p. 194.

11 Ibid., p. 309.

12 Ibid., p. 311.

13 Ibid., p. 239.

Chapter 5

1 Micheal O'Siadhail, *A Fragile City*, Newcastle-upon-Tyne, Bloodaxe, 1992, p. 68.

2 Donald Nicholl, *The Testing of Hearts. A Pilgrim's Journal*, London, Lamp Press, 1989, pp. 244–5.

3 Ibid., p. 266.

4 Ronald Hock, *The Social Context of Paul's Ministry. Tentmaking and Apostleship*, Philadelphia, Fortress Press, 1980, p. 56.

5 Perhaps the best single book is Wayne Meeks, *The First Urban Christians. The Social World of the Apostle Paul*, New Haven and London, Yale University Press, 1983.

6 Stephen R. Covey, A. Roger Merrill and Rebecca R. Merrill, *First Things First*, New York, London, Toronto, Sydney, Tokyo, Singapore, Simon and Schuster, 1994.

7 William Blake, *Milton* in *Blake, Complete Writings*, ed. Geoffrey Keynes, Oxford, Oxford University Press, 1972, pp. 480ff.

Chapter 6

1 *Letters from Baron Friedrich von Hügel to a Niece*, ed. with Introduction by Gwendolen Greene, London, J.M. Dent, 1928, pp. xv–xvi.

2 Donald Nicholl, *The Testing of Hearts. A Pilgrim's Journal*, London, Lamp Press, 1989, pp. 226–7.

3 Ibid., pp. 227–8.

4 Ibid., p. 229.

5 Micheal O'Siadhail, *Our Double Time*, due to be published 1998.

6 See above, p. 104.

7 'Threshold', in O'Siadhail, *Our Double Time*.

8 Nicholas Wolterstorff, *Lament for a Son*, Grand Rapids, Eerdmans, 1987, p. 61.

9 Ibid., p. 15.

10 Ibid., passim.

11 Ibid., p. 54.

12 Ibid., p. 81.

13 Ibid., p. 81.

14 Ibid., pp. 85–6.

15 Ibid., p. 63.

16 Sheila Cassidy, *Good Friday People*, London, Darton, Longman & Todd, 1991, p. 167.

17 Ibid., p. 170.

18 Ibid., p. 172.

19 Micheal O'Siadhail, *Hail! Madam Jazz*, Newcastle-upon-Tyne, Bloodaxe, 1992, p. 75.

Chapter 7

1 Micheal O'Siadhail, *A Fragile City*, Newcastle-upon-Tyne, Bloodaxe, 1995, p. 72.
2 Ibid., p. 73.
3 From 'Variations', in Micheal O'Siadhail, *Our Double Time*, to be published 1998.
4 Plato, *Phaedrus and the Seventh and Eighth Letters*, London, Penguin, 1973, pp. 135f.
5 *A Fragile City*, p. 75.
6 Dante Alighieri, *Paradiso*, Translated with Introduction by Allen Mandelbaum, Drawings by Barry Moser, New York, Bantam Books, 1986, p. 299.
7 Ibid., p. 301.
8 Ibid., p. 303.
9 *A Fragile City*, p. 78.

QUESTIONS FOR DISCUSSION

If this book is used for weekly discussion groups during Lent one possibility is as follows:

- Study the Introduction during the week of Ash Wednesday
- Cover chapters 1–6 during the weeks leading up to Easter
- Study chapter 7 at a final meeting after Easter

There is poetry in every chapter except the Introduction. I suggest that it be read aloud at some point during the meeting, and members encouraged to respond to it.

The questions which follow are only meant as starters. There are also suggestions for a biblical focus for thinking and meditation. In addition, it might be helpful to explore what a chapter sparks in members of the group, or to focus on particular sections of the chapter which you want to discuss in detail.

Questions on the Introduction Coping with being Overwhelmed: How Are Our Lives Shaped?

What are the main overwhelmings in our society?
Do you recognize yourself as overwhelmed? If so, in what ways?

How do you cope with being overwhelmed? Which resources are most helpful?

If you were trying to describe the shape of your life, what images would you use?

For meditation: **Ezekiel 3:14–15**

Questions on chapter 1   Faces and Voices – Shaping a Heart

Who are the most significant people in your 'community of the heart'?

Who is welcomed into your heart and who is not? Why?

What are the boundaries of yourselves or your groups that might need to be shifted?

Think about Jesus Christ being multiply overwhelmed.

How might he shape your hearts?

For meditation: **2 Corinthians 4:6**

Questions on chapter 2   Vocations and Compulsions – Life-Shaping Desires

What are the main influences shaping desires in our culture?

What does it mean to be desired by God?

Discuss the place of obedience and accountability in life.

How can our desires best be shaped?

Do the six guiding sayings about discovering your vocation ring true?

For meditation: **Psalm 27:8**

Questions on chapter 3 **Power, Virtue and Wisdom – The Shaping of Character**

What examples of real goodness have you met in recent months?
How can you receive power to be good?
Discuss some of the wisdom and wise people that have helped to shape your lives.
What can be learnt from the two stories at the end of the chapter?

For meditation: **Ephesians 3:14–21**

Questions on chapter 4 **Secrets and Disciplines – Soul-Shaping**

What are the routines and disciplines which sustain your close relationships?
What 'practices of excess' do you have which add to those routines and disciplines?
What are the routines and disciplines which sustain your relationship with God?
Discuss the role in your life, and in the life of your group or church, of the seven practices of excess (and any others).
Do you know of other communities besides L'Arche which unite suffering and celebration? What is their secret?

For meditation: **Matthew 6:6**

Questions on chapter 5   **Leisure and Work – Shaping Time and Energy**

Is 'rest before work' a sensible motto?
Discuss the ways in which your work is overwhelming and how you cope with this.
How is God involved in the network of exchanges of money, goods, services, energy, knowledge and information?
What is your 'network of membership'? Try answering some of the questions at the end of the section on this topic.
Share what you have learnt about managing your time.

For meditation: **Genesis 2:3**

Questions on chapter 6   **Knocked Out of Shape – Evil, Suffering and Death**

How have you been held in your suffering?
Who are the sufferers you have learnt most from?
What is your experience of healing?
Discuss some of Wolterstorff's questions.
Explore the meaning of Holy Saturday.

For meditation: **Luke 6:21**

Questions on chapter 7 **Kaleidoscope – Resurrection, Joy and Feasting**

Is resurrection joy a greater scandal than evil, suffering and death? Explore the practical consequences of taking a God of joy seriously.

In what ways have you tasted God's feast?

How can you feast on beauty and truth?

Is Micheal O'Siadhail's 'Dance' a good way into glimpsing the life and joy of God?

For meditation: **Ephesians 1:10**
               Philippians 4:4